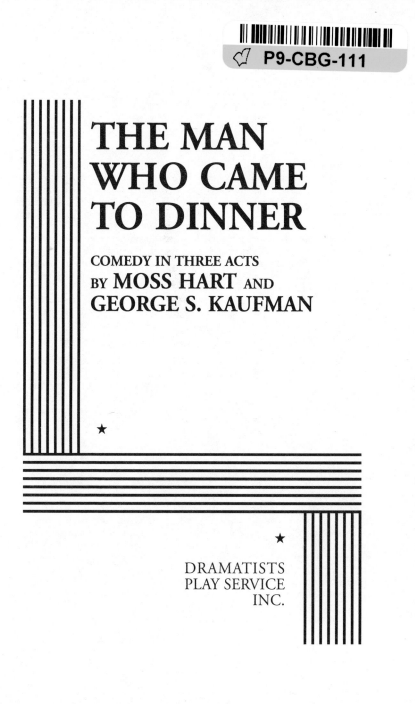

THE MAN WHO CAME TO DINNER

COMEDY IN THREE ACTS
BY **MOSS HART** AND
GEORGE S. KAUFMAN

★

★

DRAMATISTS
PLAY SERVICE
INC.

The Man Who Came to Dinner was produced by Sam H. Harris at the Music Box Theatre, New York, on Monday night, October 16, 1939, with the following cast:

MRS. ERNEST W. STANLEY	Virginia Hammond
MISS PREEN	Mary Wickes
RICHARD STANLEY	Gordon Merrick
JUNE STANLEY	Barbara Wooddell
JOHN	George Probert
SARAH	Mrs. Priestley Morrison
MRS. DEXTER	Barbara Adams
MRS. McCUTCHEON	Edmonia Nolley
MR. STANLEY	George Lessey
MAGGIE CUTLER	Edith Atwater
DR. BRADLEY	Dudley Clements
SHERIDAN WHITESIDE	Monty Woolley
HARRIET STANLEY	Ruth Vivian
BERT JEFFERSON	Theodore Newton
PROFESSOR METZ	LeRoi Operti
THE LUNCHEON GUESTS {	Phil Sheridan
	Charles Washington
	William Postance
MR. BAKER	Carl Johnson
EXPRESSMAN	Harold Woolf
LORRAINE SHELDON	Carol Goodner
SANDY	Michael Harvey
BEVERLY CARLTON	John Hoysradt
WESTCOTT	Edward Fisher
RADIO TECHNICIANS {	Rodney Stewart
	Carl Johnson
SIX YOUNG BOYS {	Daniel Leone
	Jack Whitman
	Daniel Landon
	Donald Landon
	DeWitt Purdue
	Robert Rea
BANJO	David Burns
TWO DEPUTIES {	Curtis Karpe
	Phil Sheridan
A PLAINCLOTHES MAN	William Postance

SCENE: The home of Mr. and Mrs. Stanley, in a small town in Ohio.

ACT I. SCENE 1. A December morning.
    SCENE 2. About a week later.
ACT II. Another week has passed. Christmas Eve.
ACT III. Christmas Morning.

Photo by VanDamm; courtesy of Theatre Division, New York Public Library
A scene from the original New York production of "The Man Who Came to Dinner."

THE MAN WHO CAME TO DINNER

~~~~~~

ACT ONE

SCENE 1: *The curtain rises on the attractive living-room of* MR. *and* MRS. ERNEST W. STANLEY, *in a small town in Ohio. The* STANLEYS *are obviously people of means: the room is large, comfortable, tastefully furnished. Double doors lead into a library R. There is a glimpse through an arch U.R. of a dining-room at the rear, and we see the steps of a handsome curved staircase, U.C. At the left side of the room, a bay window. Another arch, U.L. leading into the hallway. Upstage of the hallway is a swinging door leading into the pantry. The outer door to the street is off U.L. The library doors are closed.* MRS. STANLEY *enters from upstairs. As she reaches the lower third step the door-bell rings. She pauses a moment, then continues on her way towards the library. A nurse* [MISS PREEN] *in full uniform emerges—scurries rather—out of the room R., as the bell rings. An angry voice from within speeds her on her way: "Great dribbling cow!"*

MRS. STANLEY. (*Eagerly.*) How is he? Is he *coming out?*
(*But* MISS PREEN *has already disappeared into the dining-room up R. Simultaneously the door-bell rings—at the same time a young lad of twenty-one,* RICHARD STANLEY, *is descending the stairs C.*)
RICHARD. (*Crosses to door L.*) I'll go, Mother.
(JOHN, *a white-coated servant, comes hurrying in from the library and starts up the stairs, two at a time.* JOHN'S *entrance cue: follows* MISS PREEN *on her first entrance. He closes doors.*)
MRS. STANLEY. What's the matter? What is it, John?
JOHN. They want *pillows.*
(*And he is out of sight. Meanwhile* MISS PREEN *is returning to the sick-room. She enters as soon as she picks up a tray with a bowl of cornflakes, off* U.R.)
MRS. STANLEY. (*To her.*) Anything I can do, Miss Preen?

5

MISS PREEN. (*Exit to library.*) No, thank you.

(*The* VOICE *is heard again as she opens the doors. "Don't call yourself a Doctor in my presence!"* RICHARD *returns from the hall* L., *carrying two huge packages and a sheaf of cablegrams. His entrance cue is sound of library doors closing.*)

RICHARD. (*Crosses to sofa, puts packages on floor* R. *of sofa, telegrams on table back of sofa.*) Four more cablegrams and more *packages* . . . Dad is going crazy upstairs, with that bell ringing all the time.

(*Meanwhile* JUNE, *the daughter of the house, has come down stairs* C. *An attractive girl of twenty. At the same time the phone is ringing.* JUNE *crosses* D.R. *to phone.*)

MRS. STANLEY. Oh, dear! . . . June, will you go? . . . What did you say, Richard?

RICHARD. (*Examining packages.*) One's from New York and one from San Francisco.

MRS. STANLEY. There was something from Alaska early this morning. (*Before* JUNE *can answer the double doors are opened again.* MISS PREEN *appears* D.R. VOICE *calls after her: "Doesn't that bird-brain of yours ever function?"*)

RICHARD. Really?

JUNE. (*At phone.*) Yes? . . . Yes, that's right.

MRS. STANLEY. Who is it?

MISS PREEN. (*Enters* D.R. *Crosses* L.) I—I'll get them right away. . . . He wants some Players' Club cigarettes.

MRS. STANLEY. Players' Club?

(JOHN *enters from stairs* C. *with pillows. Gives pillows to* MISS PREEN D.R., *exits up* R.)

RICHARD. They have 'em at Kitchener's. I'll run down and get 'em. (*He is off* L.)

JUNE. (*Still at phone.*) Hello . . . Yes, I'm waiting.

MRS. STANLEY. (*Line cue:—"and get 'em."*) Tell me, Miss Preen, is he—are they bringing him out soon?

MISS PREEN. (*Wearily.*) We're getting him out of bed now. He'll be out very soon . . . Oh, thank you. (MISS PREEN *starts off* R.)

MRS. STANLEY. Oh, I'm so glad. He must be very happy.

(*And again we hear the invalid's* VOICE *as* MISS PREEN *passes into the room,* R. *"Trapped like a rat in this hell-hole!"*)

JUNE. (*At phone.*) Two o'clock? Yes, I think he could talk then. All right. (*She hangs up.*) Well, who do you think that was? Mr. H. G. Wells from London.

6

MRS. STANLEY. (*Wild-eyed.*) H. G. Wells? On *our telephone?*
(*The door-bell again.*)

JUNE. (*Crosses* L. *to door* L. *Exit.*) I'll go. This is certainly a *busy house.* (*Meantime* SARAH, *the cook, has come from dining-room up* R. *with a pitcher of orange juice—Entrance cue: door-bell.*)

SARAH. I got his orange juice.

MRS. STANLEY. (*As* SARAH *knocks on double doors* D.R.) Oh, that's fine, Sarah. Is it fresh?

SARAH. Yes, ma'am. (*She knocks on door. The doors are opened;* SARAH *hands orange juice to the nurse. The* VOICE *roars once more: "You move like a broken-down truck horse!"*)

SARAH. (*Beaming.*) His voice is just the same as on the radio. (*She disappears into dining-room as* JUNE *returns from entrance hall,* L., *ushering in two friends of her mother's,* MRS. DEXTER *and* MRS. MCCUTCHEON. *One is carrying a flowering plant, partially wrapped; the other is holding, with some care, what turns out to be a jar of calf's-foot jelly.*)

LADIES. (*Enter* L. *Cross to* C.) Good morning.

MRS. STANLEY. (*To them.*) Girls, what do you think? He's getting up and coming out this morning!

MRS. MCCUTCHEON. You don't mean it!

MRS. DEXTER. Can we stay and see him?

MRS. STANLEY. Why, of course—he'd love it.

(JUNE *enters* L. *Crosses to stairs.*)

Girls, do you know what just happened?

JUNE. (*Departing upstairs.*) I'll be upstairs, Mother, if you want me.

MRS. STANLEY. What? . . . Oh, yes. June, tell your father he'd better come down, will you? Mr. Whiteside is coming out.

JUNE. Yes, Mother. (*She exits upstairs.*)

MRS. DEXTER. Is he really coming out this morning? I brought him a plant—do you think it's all right if I give it to him?

MRS. STANLEY. Why, I think that would be lovely.

MRS. MCCUTCHEON. And some calf's-foot jelly.

MRS. STANLEY. Why, how nice! Who do you think was on the phone just now? H. G. Wells, from London. And look at those cablegrams. (*The* LADIES *cross* L.) He's had calls and messages from all over this country and Europe. The *New York Times*—and Felix Frankfurter, and Dr. Dafoe, the Mount Wilson Observatory —I just can't tell you what's been going on, I'm simply exhausted. (*Crosses* R., *sits chair* R.C.)

MRS. DEXTER. (*Crossing to* MRS. STANLEY R.) There's a big piece about it in this week's *Time*. Did you see it?

MRS. STANLEY. No—really?

MRS. MCCUTCHEON. (*Crosses R., gives* MRS. DEXTER *calf's-foot jelly, reads from* Time.) Your name's in it too, Daisy. Listen: "Portly Sheridan Whiteside, critic, lecturer, wit, radio orator, intimate friend of the great and near great, last week found his celebrated wit no weapon with which to combat an injured hip. The Falstaffian Mr. Whiteside, trekking across the country on one of his annual lecture tours, met his Waterloo in the shape of a small piece of ice on the doorstep of Mr. and Mrs. Ernest W. Stanley, of Mesalia, Ohio. Result: Cancelled lectures and disappointment to thousands of adoring clubwomen in Omaha, Denver, and points West. Further result: The idol of the air waves rests until further notice in home of surprised Mr. and Mrs. Stanley. Possibility: Christmas may be postponed this year." What's *that* mean?

MRS. STANLEY. (*She takes magazine: reads.*) "A small piece of ice on the doorstep of Mr. and Mrs. . . . " Think of it!

MRS. MCCUTCHEON. (*Crosses L. to sofa* D.L., *sits.*) Of course if it were *my* house, Daisy, I'd have a bronze plate put on the step, right where he fell. (MRS. DEXTER *eases back of couch.*)

MRS. STANLEY. Well, of course, I felt terrible about it. He just never goes to dinners anywhere, and he finally agreed to come here, and then *this* had to happen. Poor Mr. Whiteside! But it's going to be so wonderful having him with us, even for a little while. Just think of it! We'll sit around in the evening, and discuss books and plays, all the great people he's known. And he'll talk in that wonderful way of his. He may even read "Goodbye, Mr. Chips" to us.

(MR. STANLEY, *solid, substantial—the American business man—is descending stairs* C.)

STANLEY. (*Coming down* C.) Daisy, I can't wait any longer. If Mr. Whiteside—ah, good morning, ladies.

LADIES. Good morning.

MRS. STANLEY. (*Rises, crosses* C.) Ernest, he's coming out any minute, and H. G. Wells telephoned from London, and we're in *Time*. Look. (*She hands* Time *to* STANLEY.)

STANLEY. (*As he hands magazine back to her.*) I don't like this kind of publicity at all, Daisy. When do you suppose he's going to leave?

MRS. STANLEY. Well, he's only getting up this morning—after all, he's had quite a shock, and he's been in bed for two full weeks.

He'll certainly have to rest a few days, Ernest.

STANLEY. Well, I'm sure it's a great honor his being in the house, but it *is* a little upsetting—phone going all the time, bells ringing, messenger boys running in and out—

(*Out of the sick-room comes a business-like-looking young woman about thirty, with letters and notebook. Her name is* MARGARET CUTLER—MAGGIE *to her friends.*)

MAGGIE. (*Closing library doors.*) Pardon me, Mrs. Stanley—have the cigarettes come yet? (STANLEY *eases* U.L.)

MRS. STANLEY. (*Crosses* R.) They're on the way, Miss Cutler. My son went for them.

MAGGIE. (*Crosses* L. *to chair* R.) Thank you.

MRS. STANLEY. Ah—this is Miss Cutler, Mr. Whiteside's secretary.

MAGGIE. How do you do. May I move this chair?

MRS. STANLEY. (*All eagerness.*) You mean he's coming out now? (JOHN *appears in doorway up* R.C.)

MAGGIE. (*Moves chair up* C. *of desk. Quietly.*) He is indeed.

MRS. MCCUTCHEON. (*Rises, crosses* D.L.) He's coming out!

MRS. DEXTER. (*Crossing to* MRS. MCCUTCHEON D.L.) I can hardly wait!

MRS. STANLEY. June! June! Mr. Whiteside is coming out!

JOHN. (*Beckoning to* SARAH *off* U.R.) Sarah! Mr. Whiteside is coming out!

MRS. STANLEY. I'm so excited I just don't know what to do!

MRS. DEXTER. Me too! I know that I'll simply—

(SARAH *and* JOHN *appear in dining-room entrance,* JUNE *on stairs.* MRS. STANLEY *and the two other ladies are keenly expectant; even* STANLEY *is on the qui vive. The double doors are opened once more and* DR. BRADLEY *appears, bag in hand,* D.R. *He has taken a good deal of punishment, and speaks with a rather false heartiness.*)

MRS. STANLEY. Good morning, Dr. Bradley.

BRADLEY. Good morning, good morning. Well, here we are, merry and bright. Bring our little patient out, Miss Preen.

(*A moment's pause, and then a wheelchair is rolled through the door by the nurse. It is full of pillows, blankets, and* SHERIDAN WHITESIDE. SHERIDAN WHITESIDE *is indeed portly and Falstaffian. He is wearing an elaborate velvet smoking-jacket and a very loud tie, and he looks like every caricature ever drawn of him. There is a hush as the wheelchair rolls into the room* D.R. *Welcoming smiles break over every face. The chair comes to a halt;* WHITESIDE *looks*

9

slowly around, into each and every beaming face. His fingers drum
for a moment on the arm of the chair. He looks slowly around once
more. MAGGIE *comes* D.R. DR. BRADLEY *crosses to wheelchair, then*
MRS. STANLEY. *She laughs nervously. And then* HE *speaks.*)

WHITESIDE. (R.C., *quietly to* MAGGIE.) I may vomit.

MRS. STANLEY. (*With a nervous little laugh.*) Good morning, Mr.
Whiteside. I'm Mrs. Ernest Stanley—remember? And this is Mr.
Stanley.

STANLEY. (*Coming to* D.C.) How do you do, Mr. Whiteside? I
hope that you are better.

WHITESIDE. Thank you. I am suing you for a hundred and fifty
thousand dollars.

STANLEY. How's that? What?

WHITESIDE. I said I am suing you for a hundred and fifty thousand
dollars.

MRS. STANLEY. You mean—because you fell on our steps, Mr.
Whiteside?

WHITESIDE. Samuel J. Liebowitz will explain it to you in court. Who
are those two harpies standing there like the kiss of death? (MRS.
MCCUTCHEON, *with a little gasp, drops the calf's-foot jelly. It
smashes to the floor.*)

MRS. MCCUTCHEON. Oh, dear! My calf's-foot jelly.

WHITESIDE. Made from your own foot, I have no doubt. And now,
Mrs. Stanley, I have a few small matters to take up with you.
Since this corner druggist at my elbow tells me that I shall be con-
fined to this mouldy mortuary for at least another ten days, due
entirely to your stupidity and negligence, I shall have to carry on
my activities as best I can. I shall require the exclusive use of this
room, as well as that drafty sewer which you call the library. I want
no one to come in or out while I am in this room.

STANLEY. What do you mean, sir?

MRS. STANLEY. (*Stunned.*) We have to go up the stairs to get to
our rooms, Mr. Whiteside.

WHITESIDE. Isn't there a back entrance?

MRS. STANLEY. Why—yes.

WHITESIDE. Then use that. I shall also require a room for my secretary, Miss Cutler. Let me see. I will have a great many incoming
and outgoing calls, so please do not use the telephone. I sleep until
noon and must have quiet through the house until that hour. There
will be five for lunch today. Where is the cook?

STANLEY. Mr. Whiteside, if I may interrupt for a moment—

WHITESIDE. You may not, sir. Will you take your clammy hand off my chair? You have the touch of a sex-starved cobra! (*This last to* MISS PREEN *as she arranges his pillow.*) . . . And now will you all leave quietly, or must I ask my secretary to pass among you with a baseball bat?

(MRS. DEXTER *and* MRS. MCCUTCHEON *are beating a hasty retreat,* MRS. DEXTER'S *gift still in her hand.*)

MRS. MCCUTCHEON. Well—good-bye, Daisy. We'll call you—Oh, no, we mustn't use the phone. Well—we'll see you.

MRS. DEXTER. Good-bye. (*Both exit up* L.)

STANLEY. (*Boldly—line cue: "use the phone."*) Now look here, Mr. Whiteside—

WHITESIDE. There is nothing to discuss, sir. Considering the damage I have suffered at your hands, I am asking very little. Good day.

STANLEY. (*Controlling himself, crosses* L., *exit* L.) I'll call you from the office later, Daisy.

WHITESIDE. Not on this phone, please. (STANLEY *gives him a look, but goes.*)

WHITESIDE. Here is the menu for lunch. (*He extends a slip of paper to* MRS. STANLEY.)

MRS. STANLEY. But—I've already ordered lunch.

WHITESIDE. It will be sent up to you on a tray. I am using the dining-room for my guests . . . Where are those cigarettes?

MRS. STANLEY. (*Eases up.*) Why—my son went for them. I don't know why he—here, Sarah. Here is the menu for lunch. (*She hands* SARAH *the luncheon slip, when she has crossed to* MRS. STANLEY.) I'll—have mine upstairs on a tray. (SARAH *and* JOHN *depart up* R.)

WHITESIDE. (*To* JUNE, *who has been posed on landing during all this.*) Young lady, I cannot stand indecision. Will you either go up those stairs or come down them? (JUNE *is about to speak, decides against it and ascends stairs with a good deal of spirit.* MRS. STANLEY *is hovering uncertainly on the steps as* RICHARD *returns with cigarettes.*)

RICHARD. (*Crosses to* R.C.) Oh, good morning, Mr. Whiteside. Here are the cigarettes.—I'm sorry I was so long—I had to go to three different stores.

WHITESIDE. You were gone long enough to have a baby!

(RICHARD *is considerably taken aback. His eyes go to his mother, who motions to him to come up the stairs. They disappear together, their eyes unsteadily on* WHITESIDE.) Is there a man in the world who suffers as I do from the gross inadequacies of the human race!

11

(*To* MISS PREEN *who is fussing around chair again tucking blanket about him.*) Where are you going? Go in and read the life of Florence Nightingale and learn how unfitted you are for your chosen profession. (MISS PREEN *glares at him, but goes D.R., leaves doors open.*)

BRADLEY. (*Heartily—coming down to* L. *of chair.*) Well, I think I can safely leave you in Miss Cutler's capable hands. Shall I look in again this afternoon?

WHITESIDE. If you do, I shall spit right in your eye.

BRADLEY. Ah! What a sense of humor you writers have! By the way, it isn't really worth mentioning, but—I've been doing a little writing myself. About my medical experiences.

WHITESIDE. (*Quietly.*) Am I to be spared nothing?

BRADLEY. Would it be too much to ask you to—glance over it while you're here?

WHITESIDE. (*Eyes half closed, as though the pain were too exquisite to bear.*) Trapped.

BRADLEY. (*Delving into his bag.*) Well! I just happen to have a copy with me. (*He brings out a tremendous manuscript, places it on* WHITESIDE'S *lap.*) "The Story of an Humble Practitioner, or Forty Years an Ohio Doctor."

WHITESIDE. I shall drop everything.

BRADLEY. (*Crossing* L.) Thank you, and I hope you like it. Well, see you on the morrow. Keep that hip quiet and don't forget those little pills. Good-bye. (*He goes up* L.)

WHITESIDE. (*Annoyed at* BRADLEY.) Oh-h! (*Handing manuscript to* MAGGIE *who places it on chest* D.R.) Maggie, will you take "Forty Years Below the Navel" or whatever it's called?

MAGGIE. (*Crossing* L. *to* C., *surveying him.*) Well, I must say you have certainly behaved with all of your accustomed grace and charm.

WHITESIDE. Look here, Puss—I am in no mood to discuss my behavior, good or bad. I had no desire to cross this cheerless threshold. I was hounded and badgered into it. I now find myself, after two weeks of wracking pain, accused of behaving without charm. What would you have me do? Kiss them?

MAGGIE. (*Giving up, crossing to* WHITESIDE.) Very well, Sherry. After ten years I should have known better than to try to do anything about your manners. But when I finally give up this job I may write a book about it all. "Through the Years with Prince Charming." (*Tosses him letters.*)

WHITESIDE. Listen, Repulsive, you are tied to me with an umbilical

12

cord made of piano-wire. And now if we may dismiss the subject of my charm, for which, incidentally, I receive fifteen hundred dollars per appearance (*Enter* HARRIET L.), possibly we can go to work . . . Oh, no, we can't. Yes? (MAGGIE *crosses* R. *to* D.R. *This last is addressed to a wraith-like lady of uncertain years, who has more or less floated into the room. She is carrying a large spray of holly, and her whole manner suggests something not quite of this world.*)

HARRIET. (*Crosses to him. Her voice seems to float, too.*) My name is Harriet Stanley. I know you are Sheridan Whiteside. I saw this holly, framed green against the pine trees. I remembered what you had written about "Tess" and "Jude the Obscure." It was the nicest present I could bring you. (*She places holly in his lap, and exits upstairs* C.)

WHITESIDE. (*His eyes following her.*) For God's sake, what was that?

MAGGIE. (*Crosses* L. *to packages by sofa, takes them to chair up* R.) That was Mr. Stanley's sister, Harriet. I've talked to her a few times—she's quite strange.

WHITESIDE. Strange? She's right out of "The Hound of the Baskervilles" . . . You know, I've seen that face before somewhere.

MAGGIE. (*As she puts packages on chair* U.C.) Nonsense. You couldn't have.

WHITESIDE. (*Dismissing it.*) Oh, well! Let's get down to work. (*He hands her the armful of holly.*) Here! Press this in the Doctor's book. (MAGGIE *places holly on sofa. He picks up the first of a pile of letters.*) I see no reason why I should endorse Maiden Form Brassieres. (*He crumples up letter and drops it.*)

MAGGIE. (*Who has picked up little sheaf of messages from table back of sofa.*) Here are some telegrams.

WHITESIDE. (*A letter in his hand.*) What date is this?

MAGGIE. December tenth. (MAGGIE *sits sofa.*)

WHITESIDE. Send a wire to Columbia Broadcasting: "You can schedule my Christmas Eve broadcast from the New York studio, as I shall return East instead of proceeding to Hollywood. Stop. For special New Year's Eve broadcast will have as my guests Jascha Heifetz, Katharine Cornell, Schiaparelli, the Lunts, and Dr. Alexis Carrel, with Haile Selassie on short wave from England. Whiteside."

MAGGIE. Are you sure you'll be all right by Christmas, Sherry?

WHITESIDE. Of course I will. . . . Send a cable to Mahatma Ghandi,

Bombay, India. "Dear Boo-Boo: Schedule changed. Can you meet me Calcutta July twelfth? Dinner eight-thirty. Whiteside." Wire to editor of the *Atlantic Monthly*. "Do not worry, Stinkie. Copy will arrive. Whiteside." . . . Arturo Toscanini. Where is he?

MAGGIE. I'll find him.

WHITESIDE. "Counting on you January 4th Metropolitan Opera House my annual benefit Home for Paroled Convicts. As you know this is a very worthy cause and close to my heart. Tibbett, Rethberg, Martinelli, and Flagstad have promised me personally to appear. Will you have quiet supper with me and Ethel Barrymore afterwards? Whiteside."

(*Phone rings.* MAGGIE *crosses back of* WHITESIDE *to phone* D.R.) If that's for Mrs. Stanley, tell them she's too drunk to talk.

MAGGIE. (*At phone* D.R.) Hello . . . What? . . . Hollywood?

WHITESIDE. If it's Goldwyn, hang up.

MAGGIE. Hello Banjo! (*Her face lights up.*)

WHITESIDE. Banjo! Give me that phone!

MAGGIE. Banjo, you old so-and-so! How are you, darling?

WHITESIDE. Come on—give me that!

MAGGIE. Shut up, Sherry! . . . Are you coming East, Banjo? I miss you . . . Oh, he's going to live.

WHITESIDE. Stop driveling and give me the phone.

MAGGIE. (*Cue: "Stop driveling" cut in. Hands him phone—stands back of wheelchair.*) In fact, he's screaming at me now. Here he is.

WHITESIDE. (*Taking phone.*) How are you, you fawn's behind? And what are you giving me for Christmas? (*He roars with laughter at* BANJO'S *answer.*) What news, Banjo, my boy? How's the picture coming? . . . How are Wacko and Sloppo? . . . No, no, I'm all right . . . Yes, I'm in very good hands. I've got the best horse doctor in town . . . What about you? Having any fun? . . . Playing any cribbage? . . . What? (*Again laughs loudly.*) . . . Well, don't take all his money—leave a little bit for me. . . . You're what? . . . Having your portrait painted? By whom? Milt Gross? . . . Not really? . . . No, I'm going back to New York from here. I'll be there for twelve days, and then I go to Dartmouth for the Drama Festival. You wouldn't understand . . . Well, I can't waste my time talking to Hollywood riff-raff. Kiss Louella Parsons for me. Good-bye. (*He hangs up and turns to* MAGGIE. MAGGIE *puts phone on table* D.R.) He took fourteen hundred dollars from Sam Goldwyn at cribbage last night, and Sam said "Banjo, I will never play garbage with you again."

14

MAGGIE. (*Crossing* L. *to* L.C.) What's all this about his having his portrait painted?

WHITESIDE. M-m, Salvator Dali. (MISS PREEN *enters* D.R.) That's all that face of his needs—a Surrealist to paint it. . . . What do *you* want now, Miss Bed Fan? (MAGGIE *crosses to table back of couch* L.)

(*This is addressed to* MISS PREEN *who has returned somewhat apprehensively to the room.*)

MISS PREEN. It's—it's your pills. One every forty-five minutes. (*She drops them into his lap and hurries out of room—Exit* D.R. MAGGIE, *back of couch* L., *opens cable.*)

WHITESIDE. (*Looking after her.*) . . . Now where were we?

MAGGIE. (*The messages in her hand, crosses to* C.) Here's a cable from that dear friend of yours, Lorraine Sheldon.

WHITESIDE. Let me see it.

MAGGIE. (*Reading message, in a tone that gives* MISS SHELDON *none the better of it. Crosses to* C.) "Sherry, my poor sweet lamb, have been in Scotland on a shooting party with Lord and Lady Cunard and only just heard of your poor sweet hip." (MAGGIE *reads on.*) "Am down here in Surrey with Lord Bottomley. Sailing Wednesday on the Normandie and cannot wait to see my poor sweet Sherry. Your blossom girl, Lorraine." . . . In the words of the master, I may vomit.

WHITESIDE. Don't be bitter, Puss, just because Lorraine is more beautiful than you are.

MAGGIE. Lorraine Sheldon is a very fair example of that small but vicious circle you move in.

WHITESIDE. Pure sex jealousy if I ever saw it . . . Give me the rest of those.

MAGGIE. (*Mumbling to herself, crossing* R. *and handing him cables.*) Lorraine Sheldon . . . Lord Bottomley . . . My Aunt Fanny. (*Crossing* U.C.)

WHITESIDE. (*Who has opened next message.*) Ah! It's from Destiny's Tot.

MAGGIE. (*Crossing to* WHITESIDE. *Peering over his shoulder.*) Oh, England's little Rover Boy?

WHITESIDE. Um-hm. (*He reads.*) "Dear Baby's Breath, What is this I hear about a hip fractured in some bordello brawl? Does this mean our Hollywood Christmas Party is off? Finished the new play in Pago-Pago and it's superb. Myself and a ukulele leave Honolulu tomorrow in that order. By the way, the Sultan of Zanzi-

15

bar wants to meet Ginger Rogers. Let's face it. Oscar Wilde."

MAGGIE. (*Crossing* L. *to couch, sits.*) He does travel, doesn't he. You know, it would be nice if the world went around Beverly Carlton for a change.

WHITESIDE. Hollywood next week—why couldn't he stop over on his way to New York? Send him a cable. "Beverly Carlton, Royal Hawaiian Hotel, Honolulu." (*The door-bell rings.* WHITESIDE *is properly annoyed.*) If these people intend to have their friends using the front door . . . (JOHN *enters up* L.)

MAGGIE. What do you want them to do—use a rope ladder? (JOHN *at* L.C., *crosses to exit* L.)

WHITESIDE. I will not have a lot of mildewed pus-bags rushing in and out of this house while I am—

(*He stops as the voice of* JOHN *is heard at front door.* "Oh, good morning, Mr. Jefferson." *The answering voice of* JEFFERSON: "Good morning, John." *Roaring*—MAGGIE *rises, crosses to up* L.) There's nobody home! The Stanleys have been arrested for white-slavery! Go away!

(*But the visitor, meanwhile, has already appeared in the arch-way,* L. JEFFERSON *is an interesting-looking young man in his early thirties.*)

JEFFERSON. (*Crossing to her, back of couch.*) Good morning, Mr. Whiteside. I'm Jefferson, of the Mesalia Journal.

WHITESIDE. (*Sotto voce, to* MAGGIE.) Get rid of him.

MAGGIE. (*Brusquely.*) I'm sorry—Mr. Whiteside is seeing no one.

JEFFERSON. Really?

MAGGIE. So will you please excuse us? Good day.

JEFFERSON. (*Not giving up.*) Mr. Whiteside seems to be sitting up and taking notice.

MAGGIE. I'm afraid he's not taking notice of the Mesalia Journal. Do you mind?

JEFFERSON. (*Sizing up* MAGGIE.) You know, if I'm going to be insulted I'd like it to be by Mr. Whiteside himself. I never did like carbon copies.

WHITESIDE. (*Looking around; interested.*) M-m, touché, if I ever heard one. And in Mesalia too, Maggie dear.

MAGGIE. (*Still on the job.*) Will you please leave?

JEFFERSON. (*Ignoring her. Crosses to* C. MAGGIE *crosses to* R.C.) How about an interview, Mr. Whiteside?

WHITESIDE. I never give them. Go away.

16

JEFFERSON. Mr. Whiteside, if I don't get this interview, I lose my job.

WHITESIDE. That would be quite all right with me.

JEFFERSON. Now you don't mean that, Mr. Whiteside. You used to be a newspaper man yourself. You know what editors are like. Well, mine's the toughest one that ever lived.

WHITESIDE. You won't get around me that way. If you don't like him, get off the paper.

JEFFERSON. Yes, but I happen to think it's a good paper. William Allen White could have got out of Emporia, but he didn't.

WHITESIDE. You have the effrontery, in my presence, to compare yourself with William Allen White?

JEFFERSON. Only in the sense that White stayed in Emporia, and I want to stay here and say what I want to say.

WHITESIDE. Such as what?

JEFFERSON. (*Crossing to below couch* L.) Well, I can't put it into words, Mr. Whiteside—it'd sound like an awful lot of hooey. But the Journal was my father's paper. It's kind of a sentimental point with me, the paper. I'd like to carry on where he left off.

WHITESIDE. Ah—ahh. So you own the paper, eh?

JEFFERSON. That's right.

WHITESIDE. Then this terrifying editor, this dread journalistic Apocalypse is—you yourself?

JEFFERSON. In a word, yes.

WHITESIDE. (*Chuckles with appreciation.*) I see.

MAGGIE. (*Annoyed, starts off* R.) In the future, Sherry, let me know when you don't want to talk to people, I'll usher them right in. (*She goes into library* D.R.)

WHITESIDE. Young man . . . Come over here. I suppose you've written that novel?

JEFFERSON. (*Eases* R.) No. I've written that play.

WHITESIDE. Well, I don't want to read it. Ah, do these old eyes see a box of goodies over there? Hand them to me, will you?

JEFFERSON. (*Crossing* D.R. *to small desk table.*) The trouble is, Mr. Whiteside, that your being in this town comes under the heading of news. Practically the biggest news since the depression. So I just got to get a story. (*Crossing to* L. *of* WHITESIDE. *As he passes candy.*)

WHITESIDE. (*Examining candy.*) M-m, pecan butternut fudge.

(MISS PREEN, *on her way to kitchen with empty plate on tray, from*

17

library R. *stops short as she sees* WHITESIDE *with candy in his hand. She leaves doors open.*)

MISS PREEN. (*Crossing* D.R.) Oh, my! You mustn't eat candy, Mr. Whiteside. It's very bad for you.

WHITESIDE. (*Turning.*) My Great-aunt Jennifer ate a whole box of candy every day of her life. She lived to be a hundred and two, and when she had been dead three days she looked better than you do now. (*He swings blandly back to his visitor as he eats a candy.*) What were you saying, old fellow? You were about to say?

JEFFERSON. (*As* MISS PREEN *makes a hasty exit up* R.) I can at least report to my readers that chivalry is not yet dead.

WHITESIDE. We won't discuss it. . . . Well, now that you have won me with your pretty ways, what would you like to know?

JEFFERSON. (*Crossing in a step to* WHITESIDE.) Well, how about a brief talk on famous murders? You're an authority on murder as a fine art.

WHITESIDE. My dear boy, when I talk about murder I get paid for it. I have made more money out of the Snyder-Gray case than the lawyers did, so don't expect to get it for nothing.

JEFFERSON. Well, then, what do you think of Mesalia, how long are you going to be here, where are you going, things like that.

WHITESIDE. Very well. (A) Mesalia is a town of irresistible charm; (B) I cannot wait to get out of it, and (C) I am going from here to Crockfield, for my semi-annual visit to the Crockfield Home for Paroled Convicts, for which I have raised over half a million dollars in the last five years. From there I go to New York. Have you ever been to Crockfield, Jefferson?

JEFFERSON. No, I haven't. I always meant to.

WHITESIDE. As a newspaper man you ought to go, instead of wasting your time with me. It's only about seventy-five miles from here. Did you ever hear how Crockfield started? (*Candy box in basket on arm of his wheelchair.*)

JEFFERSON. (*Crossing* L.) No, I didn't.

WHITESIDE. Sit down, Jefferson . . . make yourself comfortable (JEFFERSON *sits on arm of couch.*) It is one of the most endearing and touching stories of our generation. One misty St. Valentine's Eve—the year was 1901—a little old lady who had given her name to an era, Victoria, lay dying in Windsor Castle. Maude Adams had not yet caused every young heart to swell as she tripped across the stage as Peter Pan; Irving Berlin had not yet written the first note of a ragtime rigadoon that was to set the nation's feet a-tapping, and

18

Elias P. Crockfield was just emerging from the State penitentiary. Destitute, embittered, cruel of heart, he wandered, on this St. Valentine's Eve, into a little church. But there was no godliness in his heart that night, no prayer upon his lips. In the faltering twilight, Elias P. Crockfield made his way toward the poor-box. With callous fingers he ripped open this poignant testimony of a simple people's faith. Greedily he clutched at the few pitiful coins within. And then a child's wavering treble broke the twilight stillness. "Please, Mr. Man," said a little girl's voice, "won't you be my Valentine?" Elias P. Crockfield turned. There stood before him a bewitching little creature of five, her yellow curls cascading over her shoulders like a golden Niagara, in her tiny outstretched hand a humble valentine. In that one crystal moment a sealed, door opened in the heart of Elias P. Crockfield, and in his mind was born an idea. Twenty-five years later three thousand ruddy-cheeked convicts were gamboling on the broad lawns of Crockfield Home, frolicking in the cool depths of its swimming pool, broadcasting with their own symphony orchestra from their own radio station. Elias P. Crockfield has long since gone to his Maker, but the little girl of the golden curls, now grown to lovely womanhood, is known as the Angel of Crockfield, for she is the wife of the *warden*.

(*Enter* MAGGIE, *stands* D.R.)

And in the main hall of Crockfield, between a Rembrandt and an El Greco, there hangs, in a simple little frame, a humble valentine.

MAGGIE. (*Who has emerged from library in time to hear the finish of this.*) And in the men's washroom, every Christmas Eve, the ghost of Elias P. Crockfield appears in one of the booths. . . . Will you sign this, please! (*Hands him letter—door-bell is heard.*)

WHITESIDE. (JEFFERSON *rises, crosses to* C.) This ageing debutante, Mr. Jefferson, I retain in my employ only because she is the sole support of her two-headed brother. (*Signs letter and hands it back to* MAGGIE.)

JEFFERSON. (*Crossing to couch for hat and starting for arch* L.) I understand . . . Well, thank you very much, Mr. Whiteside— you've been very kind. By the way, I'm a cribbage player, if you need one while you're here.

(JOHN *enters up* L.C. *crosses to hall* L.)

WHITESIDE. Fine. How much can you afford to lose?

JEFFERSON. I usually win.

WHITESIDE. We won't discuss that. Come back at eight-thirty. We'll play three-handed with Elsie Dinsmore . . .

METZ. Sherry!

WHITESIDE. Metz! (JEFFERSON *eases up stage* L. JOHN, *who has answered door-bell, has ushered in a strange-looking little man in his fifties. His hair runs all over his head and his clothes are too big for him.* JOHN *carries in a package which he places on table* D.L.) Metz, you incredible beetle-hound! What are you doing here?

METZ. (*Crossing to* C. *With a mild Teutonic accent.*) I explain, Sherry. First I kiss my little Maggie.

MAGGIE. (*Crosses to* C. *Embracing him.*) Metz darling, what a wonderful surprise!

WHITESIDE. The enchanted Metz! Jefferson, you are standing in the presence of Professor Adolph Metz, the world's greatest authority on insect life.

JEFFERSON. How do you do.

METZ. How do you do. Well, Sherry?

WHITESIDE. Metz, stop looking at me adoringly and tell me why you are here.

METZ. (*Crosses* R. *to* WHITESIDE. MAGGIE *crosses down to the* R. *of couch.*) You are sick, Sherry, so I come to cheer you.

WHITESIDE. Jefferson, he lived for two years in a cave with nothing but plant lice. He rates three pages in the Encyclopedia Britannica. Don't you, my little hookworm?

METZ. Please, Sherry, you embarrass me. Look—I have brought you a present to while away the hours. Please—(*Bringing stool at staircase to wheel-chair. He motions to* JOHN, *who carries the package to stool* L. *of wheel-chair. Package is in brown canvas cover.*) I said to my students: "Boys and girls, I want to give a present to my sick friend, Sheridan Whiteside." So you know what we did? We made for you a community of Periplaneta Americana, commonly known as the American cockroach. Behold, Sherry! Roach City! (*He strips off cover.*) Inside here are ten thousand cockroaches.

JOHN. Ten thousand—(*Headed for kitchen* U.R. *in great excitement.*) Sarah! Sarah! What do you think! (*Exits up* R.)

METZ. And in one week, Sherry, if all goes well, there will be *fifty* thousand.

MAGGIE. If all goes well—? What can go wrong? They're in there, aren't they?

WHITESIDE. (*Glaring at her.*) Quiet, please.

METZ. You can watch them, Sherry, while they live out their whole lives. Look! (JEFFERSON *crosses* C.) Here is their maternity hospital. It is fascinating. They do everything that human beings do.

MAGGIE. Well!

WHITESIDE. Please, Maggie, these are *my* cockroaches.

MAGGIE. Sorry. (*She crosses to back of* WHITESIDE'S *chair.*)

WHITESIDE. Go ahead, Metz.

METZ. With these earphones, Sherry, you listen to the mating calls. There are microphones down inside. (JEFFERSON *crosses to back of* WHITESIDE'S *chair.*) Listen! (METZ *has put earphones over* WHITE-SIDE'S *ears; he listens rapt.*)

WHITESIDE. Hmmm. How long has this been going on? (MRS. STANLEY *is seen descending stairs.*)

METZ. (*Sniffing, he crosses to* R. *and then* C. *Suddenly his face lights up.*) Aha! Periplaneta Americana! There are cockroaches in this house! (*The last addressed to* MRS. STANLEY.)

MRS. STANLEY. (*Shocked into speech.*) I beg your pardon! (WHITE-SIDE *hands earphones to* METZ. JEFFERSON *crosses* D.R. *The doorbell rings.*) Mr. Whiteside, I don't know who this man is, but I will not stand here and—

WHITESIDE. Then go upstairs. (JOHN *enters up* L. *crosses to exit* L.) These are probably my luncheon guests. Metz, you're staying for the day, of course.

METZ. Certainly.

WHITESIDE. Jefferson, stay for lunch?

JEFFERSON. Glad to. (CONVICTS *and* PRISON GUARD *enter from* U.L.)

WHITESIDE. Maggie, tell 'em there'll be two more. (MAGGIE *exits up* R.) Aw, come right in, Baker. Good morning, gentlemen. (METZ *crosses* D.R.)

(*The gentlemen addressed are three in number—two white, one black. They are convicts, and they look the part. Prison gray, handcuffed together.* BAKER, *in uniform, is a prison guard. He carries a rifle.* BAKER D.L. *of couch,* CONVICTS *back of couch.*) Jefferson, here are the fruits of that humble valentine. These men, now serving the final months of their prison terms, have chosen to enter the ivy-covered walls of Crockfield. They have come here today to learn from me a little of its tradition. . . . Gentlemen, I envy you your great adventure. (*To one of the convicts.*)

You're Michaelson, aren't you? Butcher shop murders? (CONVICTS *crossing* R. *to* C.)

MICHAELSON. Yes, sir.

WHITESIDE. Thought I recognized you. . . . The last fellow, Jeffer-

21

son— (*He lowers his tone.*) is Henderson, the hatchet fiend. Always chopped them up in a salad bowl—remember?

JEFFERSON. Oh, yes.

JOHN. (*Enter up* R.) Lunch is ready, Mr. Whiteside.

WHITESIDE. Good. Let's go right in, gentlemen. (*The* CONVICTS *and* GUARD *head for dining-room* U.R.)

JEFFERSON. (*Crossing to* WHITESIDE'S *chair.*) Can I help you?

WHITESIDE. Thank you. (*His voice rises as he is wheeled by* JEFFERSON *into dining-room, preceded by* METZ.)

We're having chicken livers Tettrazini, and Cherries Jubilee for dessert. I hope every little tummy is a-flutter with gastric *juices.* (*The curtain starts down.*) John, close the doors. I don't want a lot of people prying on their betters. (*The doors close. Only* MRS. STANLEY *is left outside. She collapses quietly against newel post.*)

CURTAIN

Medium

ACT ONE

SCENE 2: *Dining-room door open. Library door open. Late afternoon, a week later. Only a single lamp is lit.*

The room, in the week that has passed, has taken on something of the character of its occupant. Books and papers everywhere. Stacks of books on the tables, some of them just half out of their cardboard boxes. Half a dozen or so volumes, which apparently have not appealed to the Master, have been thrown onto the floor. A litter of crumpled papers around the WHITE-SIDE *wheelchair; an empty candy box has slid off his lap. An old pair of pants have been tossed over one chair, a seedy bathrobe over another. A handsome Chinese vase has been moved out of its accustomed spot and is doing duty as an ash receiver.* WHITESIDE *is in his wheelchair, asleep. Roach City is beside him, the earphones over his head. He has apparently dozed off while listening to the mating calls of Periplaneta Americana. For a moment only his rhythmic breathing is heard. Then* MISS PREEN *enters from library. She brings some medicine—a glass filled with a murky mixture. She pauses when she sees that he*

22

is asleep, then, after a good deal of hesitation, gently touches him on the shoulder. HE stirs a little; SHE musters up her courage and touches him again.

WHITESIDE. (*Slowly opening his eyes.*) I was dreaming of Lillian Russell, and I awake to find *you.* (*Takes off earphones.*)

MISS PREEN. Your—your medicine, Mr. Whiteside.

WHITESIDE. (*Taking glass.*) What time is it?

MISS PREEN. About half-past six.

WHITESIDE. Where is Miss Cutler?

MISS PREEN. She went out.

(*Enter* JOHN *up* R.)

WHITESIDE. Out?

MISS PREEN. With Mr. Jefferson. (*She goes into library, leaves doors open.* JOHN, *meanwhile, has entered from dining-room. Switch on* R. *bracket lights.*)

JOHN. All right if I turn the lights up, Mr. Whiteside?

WHITESIDE. Yes. Go right ahead, John.

JOHN. (*Crosses* L. *to switch on chandelier lights.*) And Sarah has something for you, Mr. Whiteside. Made it special.

WHITESIDE. She has? Where is she? My Soufflé Queen! (JOHN *crosses to* C.)

SARAH. (*Proudly entering with a tray on which reposes her latest delicacy, crosses down to* WHITESIDE.) Here I am, Mr. Whiteside.

WHITESIDE. She walks in beauty like the night, and in those deft hands there is the art of Michelangelo. Let me taste the new goody. (*With one hand he pours medicine into Chinese vase, then swallows at a gulp one of Sarah's not-so-little cakes. An ecstatic expression comes over his face.*) Poetry! Sheer poetry!

SARAH. (*Beaming.*) I put a touch of absinthe in the dough. Do you like it?

WHITESIDE. (*Rapturously.*) Ambrosia!

SARAH. And I got you your Terrapin Maryland for dinner.

WHITESIDE. I have known but three great cooks in my time. The Khedive of Egypt has one. My Great-aunt Jennifer another, and the third, Sarah, is you.

SARAH. Oh, Mr. Whiteside! . . .

WHITESIDE. (*Lowering his voice and beckoning to them to come closer.*) Tell me? How would you like to come to New York and work for me? You and Johnny? (JOHN *crosses* R.)

SARAH. Why, Mr. Whiteside!

23

JOHN. Sarah!

SARAH. Why, it kind of takes my breath away.

JOHN. It would be wonderful, Mr. Whiteside, but what would we say to Mr. and Mrs. Stanley?

WHITESIDE. Just "Good-bye."

SARAH. But—but they'd be awfully mad, wouldn't they? They've been very kind to us.

WHITESIDE. (*Lightly.*) Well, if they ever come to New York we can have them for dinner, if I'm not in town. Now run along and think it over. This is our little secret—just between us. And put plenty of sherry in that terrapin . . . Miss Preen! (SARAH *and* JOHN *withdraw, in considerable excitement. Up* R. WHITESIDE *raises his voice to a roar.*) Miss Preen!

MISS PREEN. (*Appearing, breathless, drying her hands.*) Yes, sir? Yes, sir?

WHITESIDE. What have you *got* in there, anyway? A sailor?

MISS PREEN. I was—just washing my hands.

WHITESIDE. What time did Miss Cutler go out?

MISS PREEN. Oh, couple hours ago.

WHITESIDE. Mr. Jefferson called for her?

MISS PREEN. Yes, sir.

WHITESIDE. (*Impatiently.*) All right, all right. Go back to your sex-life. (MISS PREEN *goes.* WHITESIDE *tries to settle down to his book, but his mind is plainly troubled. He shifts a little; looks anxiously toward outer door.* HARRIET STANLEY *comes softly down steps. She seems delighted to find* WHITESIDE *alone.*)

HARRIET. (*Opening cardboard portfolio she has brought with her—crossing down* C.) Dear Mr. Whiteside, may I show you a few mementoes of the past? I somehow feel that you would love them as I do.

WHITESIDE. I'd be delighted. (*Observing her.*)

Miss Stanley, haven't we met somewhere before?

HARRIET. Oh, no. I would have remembered. It would have been one of my cherished memories—like these. (*She spreads portfolio before him.*) Look! Here I am with my first sweetheart, under our lovely beechwood trees. I was eight and he was ten. I have never forgotten him. What happy times we had! What—(*She stops short as she hears footsteps on stairway.*)

STANLEY. (*From upstairs.*) But I tell you I'm going to.

HARRIET. There's someone coming! I'll come back! . . . (*She gathers up portfolio and vanishes into dining-room* U.R. WHITESIDE *looks after her, puzzled. It is* STANLEY *who comes down the stairs. He is plainly coming into the room for a purpose—this is no haphazard descent. He is carrying a slip of paper in his hand, and he is obviously at the boiling-point. A few steps behind comes* MRS. STANLEY, *apprehensive and nervous.*)

MRS. STANLEY. (*From stairs.*) Now, Ernest, please—

STANLEY. (*To* C.) Be quiet, Daisy . . . Mr. Whiteside, I want to talk to you. I don't care whether you're busy or not. I have stood all that I'm going to stand.

WHITESIDE. Indeed?

STANLEY. This is the last straw. I have just received a bill from the telephone company for seven hundred and eighty-four dollars. (*He reads from slip in his hand.*) Oklahoma City, Calcutta, Hollywood, Australia, Rome, New York, New York, New York, New York.— (*His voice trails off in an endless succession of New Yorks.*) Now I realize, Mr. Whiteside, that you are a distinguished man of letters—

MRS. STANLEY. (C.) Yes, of course, we both do.

STANLEY. Please . . . But in the past week we have not been able to call our souls our own. We have not had a meal in the dining-room *once*. I have to tiptoe out of the house in the mornings.

MRS. STANLEY. Now, Ernest—

STANLEY. (*Waving her away.*) Oh, I come home to find convicts sitting at my dinner-table—butcher-shop murderers. A man putting cockroaches in the kitchen.

MRS. STANLEY. They just escaped, Ernest.

STANLEY. That's not the point. I go into my bathroom and bump into twenty-two Chinese students that you invited here. I tell you I won't stand for it, no matter *who* you are.

WHITESIDE. Have you quite finished?

STANLEY. No, I have not. I go down into the cellar this morning and trip over that octopus that William Beebe sent you. I tell you I won't stand it. Mr. Whiteside, I want you to leave this house— (MRS. STANLEY *starts to tap* STANLEY'S *shoulder.*) as soon as you can, and go to a hotel. . . . Stop pawing me, Daisy . . . That's all I've got to say, Mr. Whiteside.

WHITESIDE. And quite enough, I should think. May I remind you again, Mr. Stanley, that I am not a willing guest in this house. I am informed by my doctor that I must remain quiet for another ten days, at which time I shall get out of here so fast that the wind will knock you over, I hope. If, however, you insist on my leaving before that, thereby causing me to suffer a relapse, I shall sue you for every additional day that I am held inactive, which will amount I assure you, to a tidy sum.

STANLEY. (*To* MRS. STANLEY.) This is outrageous. Outrageous!—

WHITESIDE. As for the details of your petty complaints, those twenty-two Chinese students came straight from the White House, where I assure you they used the bathroom, too!

MRS. STANLEY. Mr. Whiteside, my husband didn't mean—

STANLEY. Yes, I did. I meant every word of it.

WHITESIDE. There is only one point that you make in which I see some slight justice. I do not expect you to pay for my telephone calls, and I shall see to it that restitution is made. Can you provide me with the exact amount?

STANLEY. I certainly can, and I certainly will.

WHITESIDE. Good. I shall instruct my lawyers to deduct it from the hundred and fifty thousand dollars that I am suing you for. (STANLEY *starts to speak, but simply chokes with rage. Furious, he storms up steps again.*)

MRS. STANLEY. (*Following.*) Now, Ernest—

WHITESIDE. (*Calling after him.*) And I'll thank you not to trip over that octopus, which once belonged to Chauncey Depew.

MRS. STANLEY. You—you mustn't get excited. Remember Mr. Whiteside is a guest here. (*Exit upstairs. Left alone,* WHITESIDE *enjoys his triumph for a moment, then his mind jumps to more important matters. He looks at his watch, considers a second, then wheels himself over to the telephone.*)

WHITESIDE. Give me the Mesalia Journal, please. (*He peers at Roach City while waiting, then taps peremptorily on the glass.*) Hello, Journal? . . . Is Mr. Jefferson there? . . . When do you expect him? (RICHARD *and* JUNE *enter* U.L.) No. No message. (*He hangs up; drums impatiently on arm of his chair. Then he turns sharply at sound of outer door opening. But it is the younger* STANLEY'S, RICHARD *and* JUNE, *who enter. They are in winter togs, with ice-skates under their arms. In addition,* RICHARD *has a camera slung over his shoulder. Their attitudes change as they see that* WHITESIDE *is in the room.* THEY *slide toward stairs, obviously trying to be as unobtrusive as possible. Enter* L., *crossing up, then down* C.) Come here, you two. . . . Come on, come on. I'm not going to bite you . . . Now look here. I am by nature a gracious and charming person. If I veer at it, it is on the side of kindness and amiability—I have been observing you two for this past week, and you seem to me to be extremely likable young people. I am afraid that when we first met I was definitely unpleasant to you. For that I am sorry, and I wish that in the future you would not treat me like something out of Edgar Allan Poe. How do you like my new tie?

JUNE. (C.) Thank you, Mr. Whiteside. This makes things much pleasanter. And I think the tie is very pretty.

RICHARD. Well, now that we're on speaking terms, Mr. Whiteside, I don't mind telling you that I have been admiring all your ties.

WHITESIDE. Do you like this one?

RICHARD. I certainly do.

WHITESIDE. It's yours. (*He takes it off and tosses it to him.*)

RICHARD. (*Crosses* R.) Oh, thank you.

WHITESIDE. Really, this curious legend that I am a difficult person is pure fabrication. . . . Ice-skating, eh? Ah, me! I used to cut figure eights myself, arm in arm with Betsy Ross, waving the flag behind us.

JUNE. It was wonderful on the ice today. Miss Cutler and Mr. Jefferson were there.

WHITESIDE. Maggie? Ice-skating?

RICHARD. Yes, and she's good, too. I got a marvelous picture of her.

WHITESIDE. Were they still there when you left?

RICHARD. I think so.

JUNE. Yes, they were.

RICHARD. Mr. Whiteside, mind if I take a picture of you? I'd love to have one.

WHITESIDE. Very well. Do you want my profile? (*He indicates his stomach.*)

JUNE. (*Starting up stairs.*) I'm afraid you're done for, Mr. White-side. My brother is a camera fiend. (WHITESIDE, *slightly startled, turns his head sharply, and in that instant* RICHARD *clicks camera.*)

RICHARD. Thank you, Mr. Whiteside. I got a great one. (*He and* JUNE *go up stairs as* MAGGIE *enters from hallway. They call* "Hello, Miss Cutler!" *as they disappear upstairs.*)

MAGGIE. (*Enters* L., *puts bag and gloves on table back of couch.*) Hello there . . . Good evening, Sherry. Really, Sherry, you've got this room looking like an old parrot-cage . . . Did you nap while I was out? (*Crossing* R. *to* C. WHITESIDE *merely glowers at her.*) What's the matter, dear? Cat run away with your tongue?

WHITESIDE. (*Furious.*) Don't look at me with those great cow-eyes, you sex-ridden hag. Where have you been all afternoon? Alley-catting around with Bert Jefferson?

27

MAGGIE. (*Her face aglow, crossing to him.*) Sherry, Bert read his play to me this afternoon. It's superb. It isn't just that play written by a newspaperman. It's superb. (*To him.*) I want you to read it tonight. (*She puts it in his lap.*) It just cries out for Cornell. Will you send it to her, Sherry? And will you read it tonight?

WHITESIDE. No, I will not read it tonight or any other time. And while we're on the subject of Mr. Jefferson, you might ask him if he wouldn't like to pay your salary, since he takes up all your time.

MAGGIE. (*She is on her knees, gathering up debris L. of wheelchair.*) Oh, come now, Sherry. It isn't as bad as that.

WHITESIDE. I have not even been able to reach you, not knowing what haylofts you frequent.

MAGGIE. (*Crossing to back of sofa with box of debris.*) Oh, stop behaving like a spoiled child, Sherry.

WHITESIDE. Don't take that patronizing tone with me, you flea-bitten Cleopatra. I am sick and tired of your sneaking out like some love-sick high-school girl every time my back is turned.

MAGGIE. Well, Sherry—I'm afraid you've hit the nail on the head. (*Taking off hat and putting it on table back of couch.*)

WHITESIDE. Stop acting like Zazu Pitts and explain yourself.

MAGGIE. (*To C.*) I'll make it quick, Sherry. I'm in love.

WHITESIDE. Nonsense. This is merely delayed puberty.

MAGGIE. No, Sherry, I'm afraid this is it. You're going to lose a very excellent secretary.

WHITESIDE. You are out of your mind.

MAGGIE. Yes, I think I am, a little. But I'm a girl who's waited a long time for this to happen, and now it has. Mr. Jefferson doesn't know it yet, but I'm going to try my darnedest to marry him. (*Ease L.*)

WHITESIDE. (*As she pauses.*) Is that all?

MAGGIE. Yes, except that—well—I suppose this is what might be called my resignation, as soon as you've got someone else.

WHITESIDE. (*A slight pause.*) Now listen to me, Maggie. We have been together for a long time. You are indispensable to me, but I think I am unselfish enough not to let that stand in the way where your happiness is concerned. Because whether you know it or not, I have a deep affection for you.

MAGGIE. (*Ease R.*) I know that, Sherry.

WHITESIDE. That being the case, I will not stand by and allow you to make a fool of yourself.

MAGGIE. I'm not, Sherry.

WHITESIDE. You are, my dear. You are behaving like a Booth Tarkington heroine. It's—it's incredible. I cannot believe that a girl who for the past ten years has had the great of the world served up on a platter before her, I cannot believe that it is anything but a kind of temporary insanity when you are swept off your feet in seven days by a second-rate, small-town newspaper man.

MAGGIE. (*To him.*) Sherry, I can't explain what's happened. I can only tell you that it's so. It's hard for me to believe, too, Sherry. Here I am, a hard-bitten old cynic, behaving like True Story Magazine, and liking it. Discovering the moon, and ice-skating—I keep laughing to myself all the time, but there it is. What can I do about it, Sherry? I'm in love.

WHITESIDE. (*With sudden decision.*) We're leaving tomorrow. Hip or no hip, we're leaving here tomorrow. I don't care if I fracture the other one. Get me a train schedule and start packing. I'll pull you out of this, Miss Stardust. *I'll* get the ants out of those moonlit pants.

MAGGIE. (*Crosses* L.) It's no good, Sherry. It's no good. I'd be back on the next streamlined train.

WHITESIDE. It's completely unbelievable. Can you see yourself, the wife of the editor of the Mesalia Journal, having an evening at home for Mr. and Mrs. Stanley, Mr. and Mrs. Poop-Face, and the members of the Book-of-the-Month Club?

MAGGIE. (*Crosses* R.) Sherry, I've had ten years of the great figures of our time, and don't think I'm not grateful to you for it. I've loved every minute of it. They've been wonderful years, Sherry. Gay, and stimulating—I don't think anyone has ever had the fun we've had. But a girl can't laugh all the time, Sherry. There comes a time when she wants—Bert Jefferson. You don't know Bert, Sherry. He's gentle and he's unassuming, and—well, I love him, that's all. (*Ease* L.)

WHITESIDE. I see. Well, I remain completely unconvinced. You are drugging yourself into this Joan Crawford fantasy, and before you become completely anesthetized I shall do everything in my power to bring you to your senses.

MAGGIE. (*Wheeling on him.*) Now listen to me, Whiteside. I know you. Lay off. I know what a devil you can be. I've seen you do it to other people, but don't you dare do it to me. Don't drug *yourself* into the idea that all you're thinking of is my happiness. You're thinking of yourself a little bit, too, and all those months of breaking in somebody new. I've seen you in a passion before when your life has been disrupted, and you couldn't dine in Calcutta on July twelfth with Boo-Boo. Well, that's too bad, but there it is. (*Crosses to stairs.*) I'm going to marry Bert if he'll have me, and don't you dare try any of your tricks. I'm on to every one of them. So lay off. That's my message to you, Big Lord Fauntleroy. (*And she is up the stairs.*) (*Left stewing in his own juice,* WHITESIDE *is in a perfect fury. He bangs arm of his chair, then slaps at manuscript in his lap. As he does so, the dawn of an idea comes into his mind. He sits perfectly still for a moment, thinking it over. Then, with a slow smile, he takes manuscript out of its envelope. He looks at title page, ruffles through the script, then stops and thinks again. His face breaks out into one great smile. He reaches for phone receiver.*)

WHITESIDE. (*In a lowered voice, meanwhile discarding cables from basket until he finds right one.*) Long distance, please. I want to put in a Transatlantic call. (*He looks at cablegram again for confirmation.*) Hello. Transatlantic operator? . . . This is Mesalia 1–4–2. I want to talk to Miss Lorraine Sheldon—S-h-e-l-d-o-n. She's on the Normandie. It sailed from Southampton day before yesterday. (*Door-bell.*) Will it take long? . . . All right. My name is Whiteside . . . thank you.

(*He hangs up. He goes back to manuscript again and looks through it.* JOHN *then ushers in* DR. BRADLEY.)

BRADLEY. (*Offstage.*) Good evening, John.

JOHN. Good evening, Doctor. (*Exits swinging-door* U.L.)

BRADLEY. (*Crosses to* R.) (*Heartily as usual.*) Well, well! Good evening, Mr. Whiteside!

WHITESIDE. Come back tomorrow—I'm busy.

BRADLEY. (*Turning cute.*) Now what would be the best news that I could possibly bring you?

WHITESIDE. You have hydrophobia.

BRADLEY. (*Laughing it off.*) No, no . . . Mr. Whiteside, you are a well man. You can get up and walk *now*. You can leave here tomorrow.

WHITESIDE. What do you mean?

BRADLEY. (*Ease* R.) Well, sir! I looked at those X-rays again this afternoon, and do you know what? I had been looking at the wrong X-rays. I had been looking at old Mrs. Moffat's X-rays. You are perfectly, absolutely well!

WHITESIDE. Lower your voice, will you?

BRADLEY. What's the matter? Aren't you pleased?

WHITESIDE. Delighted . . . naturally . . . Ah—this is a very unexpected bit of news, however. It comes at a very curious moment. (*He is thinking fast; suddenly he gets an idea. He clears his throat and looks around apprehensively.*) Dr. Bradley, I—ah—have some good news for you, too. I have been reading your book —ah—"Forty Years"—what is it?

BRADLEY. (*Eagerly crossing to* WHITESIDE.) "An Ohio Doctor"— Yes.

WHITESIDE. I consider it extremely close to being one of the great literary contributions of our time.

BRADLEY. Mr. Whiteside!

WHITESIDE. So strongly do I feel about it, Dr. Bradley, that I have a proposition to make to you. Just here and there the book is a little uneven, a little rough, and what I would like to do is to stay here in Mesalia and work with you on it.

BRADLEY. (*All choked up.*) Mr. Whiteside, I would be so terribly honored—

WHITESIDE. Yes. But there is just one difficulty. You see, if my lecture bureau and my radio sponsors were to learn that I am well, they would insist on my fulfilling my contracts, and I would be forced to leave Mesalia. Therefore we must not tell anyone—not anyone at all—that I am well.

BRADLEY. I see. I see.

WHITESIDE. Not even Miss Cutler, you understand.

BRADLEY. No, I won't. Not a soul. Not even my wife.

WHITESIDE. That's fine.

BRADLEY. Mr. Whiteside. When do we start work—tonight? I've got just one patient that's dying and then I'll be *perfectly free.* (*Phone rings.*)

WHITESIDE. (*Waving him away—Doctor starts to go.*) Ah—tomorrow morning. This is a private call—would you forgive me? . . . Hello . . . Yes, I'm on. (*He turns again to Doctor.*) Tomorrow morning.

BRADLEY. Tomorrow morning it is. Goodnight. I'll be so proud to work with you. You've made me very proud, Mr. Whiteside. (*He exits up* L.)

WHITESIDE. Yes, yes, I know—very proud. (*Again on phone.*) Yes, yes, this is Mr. Whiteside on the phone. Put them through . . . Hello. Is this my Blossom Girl? How are you, my lovely? . . . No, no, I'm all right . . . Yes, still out here . . . Lorraine dear, when do you land in New York? . . . Tuesday? That's fine

31

. . . Now listen closely, my pet. I've great news for you. I've discovered a wonderful play with an enchanting part in it for you. Cornell would give her eye-teeth to play it, but I think I can get it for you. . . . Now wait, wait. Let me tell you. The author is a young newspaper man in this town. Of course he wants Cornell, but if you jump on a train and get out here, I think you could swing it, if you play your cards right. . . . No, he's young, and very attractive, and just your dish, my dear. It just takes a little doing, and you're the girl that can do it. Isn't that exciting, my pet? . . . Yes . . . Yes, that's right . . . And look. Don't send me any messages. Just get on the train and arrive . . . Oh, no, don't thank me, my darling. It's perfectly all right. Have a nice trip and hurry out here. Good-bye, my blossom. (*He hangs up and looks guiltily around. Then he straightens up and gleefully rubs his hands together.* MISS PREEN *enters* D.R., *medicine in hand, and frightened, as usual.*) (WHITESIDE, *jovial as hell.*) Hello, Miss Preen. God, you're looking radiant this evening! (*He takes medicine from her and swallows it at one gulp.* MISS PREEN, *staggered, retreats into library* D.R., *just as* MAGGIE *comes down stairs. She is dressed for the street.*)

MAGGIE. (*Pausing on landing, crossing to* C.) Sherry, I'm sorry for what I said before. I'm afraid I was a little unjust.

WHITESIDE. (*All nobility.*) That's all right, Maggie dear. We all lose our tempers now and then.

MAGGIE. I promised to have dinner with Bert and go to a movie, but we'll come back and play cribbage with you instead.

WHITESIDE. Fine.

MAGGIE. See you soon, Sherry dear. (*She kisses him lightly on the forehead and goes on her way. Exit* L.) Good-bye.

WHITESIDE. Good-bye. (WHITESIDE *looks after her until he hears doors close. Then his face lights up again and he bursts happily into song as he wheels himself into library.*)

"I'se des' a 'ittle wabbit in the sunshine,

(*Curtain starts down.*)

I'se des' a 'ittle wabbit in the rain.

I nibble on my lettuce-leaf all morning—"

CURTAIN

(*Medium*)

ACT TWO

Scene is the same.

A week later, late afternoon.

The room is now dominated by a large Christmas tree, set in the curve of the staircase, and hung with customary Christmas ornaments. JOHN *is standing at* L. *of tree.* SARAH *and* JOHN *are passing in and out of library, bringing forth huge packages which they are placing under tree.* MAGGIE *sits at a little table* D.R., *going through a pile of correspondence.*

JOHN. (*To tree, then* D.R.) Well, I guess that's all there are, Miss Cutler. They're all under the tree.

MAGGIE. Thank you, John.

SARAH. My, I never saw anyone get so many presents. I can hardly wait to see what's in 'em.

JOHN. When'll Mr. Whiteside open them, Miss Cutler?

MAGGIE. (*Rises, crosses to table back of sofa with papers—first switching on lights.*) Well, John, you see Christmas is Mr. Whiteside's personal property. He invented it and it belongs to *him.* First thing tomorrow morning Mr. Whiteside will open each and every present and there will be the God-damnedest fuss you ever saw.

SARAH. (*Turns on* C. *lamp and crossing to* R. *of tree.* JOHN *crosses to* L. *of tree. Then bending over packages.*) My, look who he's got presents from! Shirley Temple, William Lyon Phelps, Billy Rose, Ethel Waters, Somerset Maugham—my, I can hardly wait for *tomorrow.* (MAGGIE *crosses* R. *to* D.R. *desk. Sits.*) (*The doorbell rings.* JOHN *departs for door* L., *switching on lights on his way.* SARAH *comes downstage.*) My it certainly is wonderful. And Mr. Whiteside's tree is so beautiful, too. Mr. and Mrs. Stanley had to put theirs in their bedroom, you know. They can hardly *undress at night.* (*It is* BERT JEFFERSON *who enters* L.)

BERT. Good evening, John.

JOHN. Good evening, Mr. Jefferson, Merry Christmas.

BERT. Hello, Maggie. Merry Christmas, Sarah.

SARAH. Merry Christmas, Mr. Jefferson. (SARAH *disappears into dining-room.* JOHN *exits up* L.)

BERT. (*Crossing to* C.) (*Observing pile of packages under tree.*) Say, business is good, isn't it? My, what a little quiet blackmail and

33

a weekly radio hour can get you. What did his sponsors give him?

MAGGIE. They gave him a full year's supply of their product—Cream of Mush.

BERT. Well he'll give it right back to them, over the air.

MAGGIE. (*Rises, crosses to couch with papers.*) Wait until you hear tonight's broadcast, old fellow. It's so sticky I haven't been able to get it off my fingers since I copied it.

BERT. (*To C.*) I'll bet. . . . Look, I'll come clean. Under the influence of God knows what I have just bought you a Christmas present.

MAGGIE. (*Surprised, crossing to him.*) Why, Mr. Jefferson, sir.

BERT. Only I'd like you to see it before I throw away my hard-earned money. Can you run downtown with me and take a look at it?

MAGGIE. (*To him.*) Bert, this is very sweet of you. I'm quite touched. What is it? I can't wait.

BERT. A two years' subscription to Pic, Click, and Look and Listen. Say, do you think I'm going to tell you? Come down and see.

MAGGIE. (*Crosses R., then to L. to get coat.*) All right.
(*She calls into library.*)
Sherry! I'm going out for a few minutes. With Horace Greeley. I won't be long. (*She goes into hallway for her coat and hat.*)

BERT. (*Raising his voice.*) Noel, Noel, Mr. W.! How about some cribbage after your broadcast tonight? (*Crossing to* WHITESIDE. *The Whiteside wheelchair is rolled in by* MISS PREEN, D.R. *She then exits* D.R., *closing doors.*)

WHITESIDE. (R.C.) No, I will not play cribbage with you, Klondike Harry . . . Where are you off to now, Madam Butterfly?

MAGGIE. (*To C.*) I'm being given a Christmas present. Anything you want done downtown?

WHITESIDE. Yes. Bring baby a lollipop . . . What are *you* giving me for Christmas, Jefferson? I have enriched your feeble life beyond your capacity to repay me.

BERT. Yes, that's what I figured, so I'm not giving you anything.

WHITESIDE. I see. Well, I was giving you my old truss, but now I shan't . . . (BERT *eases upstage.*) Maggie, what time are those radio men coming?

MAGGIE. (*Crosses D.R., places phone on stool beside* WHITESIDE.) About six-thirty—I'll be here. You've got to cut, Sherry. You're four minutes over. Oh, by the way, there's a wire here from Beverly Carlton. He doesn't know what train he can get out of Chicago, but he'll be here some time this evening.

WHITESIDE. Good! Is he staying over night?

MAGGIE. (*At desk.*) No, he has to get right out again. He's sailing Friday on the Queen Mary.

BERT. (*Crossing to* WHITESIDE.) Think I could peek in at the window and get a look at him? Beverly Carlton used to be one of my heroes. (MAGGIE *puts letters and book on stool too.*)

WHITESIDE. Used to be, you ink-stained hack? Beverly Carlton is the greatest single talent in the English theatre today.—Take this illiterate numbskull out of my sight, Maggie, and don't bring him back.

BERT. Yes, Mr. Whiteside, sir. I won't come back until Beverly Carlton gets here.

MAGGIE. (*Crossing* L. *to exit* L. *As they go on their way, arm-in-arm.*) Where are we going, Bert? I want to know what you've bought me—I'm like a ten-year-old kid.

BERT. (*Laughing a little.*) You know, you look like a ten-year-old kid right now, Maggie, at that. (*They are out of earshot by this time.* WHITESIDE *looks after them intently; listens until the door closes. He considers for a second, then wheels himself over to phone.*)

WHITESIDE. (*On phone.*) Will you give me the Mansion House, please—No, I don't know the number . . . Hello? Mansion House? . . . Tell me, has a Miss Lorraine Sheldon arrived yet? . . . Yes, that's right—Miss Lorraine Sheldon. From New York . . . She hasn't, eh?

(*He hangs up; drums with his fingers on chair arm; looks at his watch. He slaps his knees impatiently, stretches. Then, vexed at his self-imposed imprisonment, he looks cautiously around room, peers up stairs. Then, slowly, he gets out of his chair, crosses* L. *and indulges in a few mild dance-steps, looking cautiously around all the while.*)

(*Then the sound of library doors being opened sends him scurrying back to his chair. It is* MISS PREEN *who emerges* D.R., *carrying basin with hot-water bag, inhalator.*)

(WHITESIDE, *annoyed.*) What do you want, coming in like that? Why don't you knock before you come into a room?

MISS PREEN. (*Crossing down to* R. *of wheelchair.*) But—I wasn't coming in. I was coming out.

WHITESIDE. Miss Preen, you are obviously *in* this room. That is true, isn't it?

MISS PREEN. Yes, it is, but—

35

WHITESIDE. Therefore you *came in.* (*Before* MISS PREEN *can reply, however,* JOHN *enters from dining-room up* R. *crosses* L. *to exit* L.) Hereafter, please knock.

JOHN. (*En route to front door up* L.) There're some expressmen here with a crate, Mr. Whiteside. I told them to come around the front.

WHITESIDE. Thank you, John . . . Don't stand there, Miss Preen. You look like a frozen custard. Go away.

MISS PREEN. (*Controlling herself as best she can.*) Yes, sir. (*She exits up* R. *At the same time an* EXPRESSMAN *carrying a crate enters from front door.*)

JOHN. (*Up* L.) Bring it right in here. Careful there—don't scrape the wall. Why, it's some kind of animals.

(*Enter* EXPRESSMAN *to up* L.)

EXPRESSMAN. (*Crossing* R. *to up* C.) I'll say it's animals. We had to feed 'em at seven o'clock this morning.

WHITESIDE. Who's it from, John?

JOHN. (*Crossing* R.) (*Reading from top of crate as they set it down.*) Admiral Richard E. Byrd. Say!

WHITESIDE. Bring it over here. (EXPRESSMAN *carries it to chair.* JOHN *crosses to chair.*)

(*Peering through slats.*) Why, they're penguins. Two—three—four penguins. Hello, my pretties.

EXPRESSMAN. (*Crossing* L.) Directions for feeding are right on top. Two of those slats are loose.

JOHN. (*Reading.*) "To be fed only whale blubber, eels and cracked lobster."

EXPRESSMAN. They got Coca-Cola this morning. And liked it. (*He goes* L.)

WHITESIDE. (*Peering through slats again.*) Hello, hello, hello. You know, they make the most entrancing companions, John. I want these put right in the library with me. Take 'em right in.

JOHN. (*Crossing* R., *exits* D.R.) (*Picking up crate.*) Yes, sir.

WHITESIDE. Better tell Sarah to order a couple of dozen lobsters.

JOHN. Yes, sir.

WHITESIDE. I don't suppose there's any whale blubber in this town.
. . . .

BRADLEY. (*Enters* L.) Good evening.

WHITESIDE. Oh, yes, there is. (*This last is addressed to* BRADLEY, *who has entered from hall as* JOHN *and crate disappear into library.*)

BRADLEY. The door was open, so I—Merry Christmas. (*Crosses to* C.)

WHITESIDE. Merry Christmas, Merry Christmas. Do you happen to know if eels are in season, Doctor?

BRADLEY. How's that?

WHITESIDE. Never mind. I was a fool to ask you. (JOHN *returns from library, carefully closing doors.*)

JOHN. (*Crossing upstairs.*) I opened those two slats a little, Mr. Whiteside—they seemed so crowded in there.

WHITESIDE. Thank you, John.

BRADLEY. Mr. Whiteside— (JOHN *goes on his way, carrying pillow-cases.*)

WHITESIDE. Good-bye, Doctor. I'm sorry you happened to drop in now. I have to do my Yogi exercises. (*He folds his arms, leans back and closes his eyes.*)

BRADLEY. But, Mr. Whiteside, it's been a week now. My book—you know—when are we going to start work on my book? (WHITESIDE *places fingers to his lips.*) I was hoping that today, maybe— (*He stops as* MISS PREEN *enters from* U.R.) Good evening, Miss Preen.

MISS PREEN. Good evening, Doctor Bradley. (*She opens door into library, then freezes in her tracks. She closes the doors again and turns to* BRADLEY, *glassy-eyed. She raises a trembling hand to her forehead, and goes to* R. *of chair.*) Doctor, perhaps I'm not well—but,—when I opened the doors just now I thought I saw a penguin with a thermometer in his mouth.

WHITESIDE. What's this? Have those penguins gotten out of their crate?

MISS PREEN. Penguins? Did you say penguins?

WHITESIDE. Yes. Doctor, will you go in and capture them, please, and put them back in the crate. There're four of them.

BRADLEY. (*Crosses* R.) Capture the penguins, yes! (JOHN'S *entrance cue.*)

WHITESIDE. Yes. And, Miss Preen, will you entertain them, please, until I come in? (*She crosses to door* R.)

MISS PREEN. (*Swallowing hard.*) Yes, sir.

JOHN. (*Descending the stairs.*) The Christmas tree in the bedroom just fell on Mr. Stanley. He's got a big bump on his forehead. (JOHN *exits* U.R.)

WHITESIDE. (*Brightly.*) Why, isn't that too bad? (RICHARD *enters from hall* L. *as* MISS PREEN *goes through library door.*) . . . Go ahead, Doctor. Go on, Miss Preen.

RICHARD. (*Coming* C.) Hello, Mr. Whiteside.

WHITESIDE. Hello, Dickie, my boy.

BRADLEY. Well, Mr. Whiteside, will you have some time later?

WHITESIDE. I don't know, Doctor. I'm busy now.

BRADLEY. Well, suppose I wait a little while? I'll—I'll wait a little while. (*Exit* BRADLEY *into library.*)

WHITESIDE. Dr. Bradley is the greatest living argument for mercy killings. Well, Dickie, would you like a candid camera shot of my left nostril this evening?

RICHARD. I'm all stocked up on those. Have you got a minute to look at some new ones I've taken? (*He hands him snap-shots.* RICHARD *crosses* U. *to ottoman, places ottoman* L. *of wheelchair.*)

WHITESIDE. I certainly have . . . why, these are splendid, Richard. There's real artistry in them—they're as good as anything by Margaret Bourke White. (RICHARD *sits.*) I like all the things you've shown me. This is the essence of photographic journalism.

RICHARD. Say, I didn't know they were as good as that. I just like to take pictures, that's all.

WHITESIDE. Richard, I've been meaning to talk to you about this. You're not just a kid fooling with a camera any more. These are good. This is what you ought to do. (*Handing back pictures.*) You ought to get out of here and do some of the things you were telling me about. Just get on a boat and get off wherever it stops. Galveston, Mexico, Singapore—work your way through and just take pictures—millions of them, terrible pictures, wonderful pictures—everything.

RICHARD. Say, wouldn't I like to, though! It's what I've been dreaming of for years. If I could do that I'd be the happiest guy in the world.

WHITESIDE. Well, why can't you do it? If I were your age, I'd do it like a shot.

RICHARD. (*Rises, crosses* L.) Well, you know why. Dad.

WHITESIDE. Richard, do you really want to do this more than anything else in the world?

RICHARD. I certainly do.

WHITESIDE. Then do it. (JUNE *enters up* R. *to* C.)

JUNE. Hello, Dick. Good afternoon, Mr. Whiteside.

WHITESIDE. Hello, my lovely . . . So I'm afraid it's up to you, Richard.

RICHARD. (*Crossing to stairs.*) I guess it is. Well, thank you, Mr.

38

Whiteside. You've been swell and I'll never forget it.

WHITESIDE. Righto, Richard.

RICHARD. (WHITESIDE *takes book from ottoman.*) June, are you coming upstairs?

JUNE. Ah—in a few minutes, Richard.

RICHARD. Well—knock on my door, will you? I want to talk to you. (*Exits upstairs.*)

JUNE. Yes, I will. (*Turning back to* WHITESIDE.) Mr. Whiteside . . .

WHITESIDE. June, my lamb, you were too young to know about the Elwell murder, weren't you? Completely fascinating. I have about five favorite murders and the Elwell case is one of them. Would you like to hear about it?

JUNE. Well, Mr. Whiteside, I wanted to talk to you. Would you mind, for a few minutes? It's important.

WHITESIDE. Why, certainly, my dear. I take it this is all about your young Lothario at the factory?

JUNE. (*Nodding.*) Yes. I just can't seem to make Father under·stand. It's like talking to a blank wall. He won't meet him—he won't even talk about it. What are we going to do, Mr. Whiteside? Sandy and I love each other. I don't know where to turn.

WHITESIDE. My dear, I'd like to meet this young man. I'd like to see him for myself.

JUNE. Would you, Mr. Whiteside? Would you meet him? He's —he's outside now. He's in the kitchen. (*Crosses up a little.*)

WHITESIDE. Good! Bring him in.

JUNE. (*Then down to* WHITESIDE *again.*) Mr. Whiteside, he's— he's a very sensitive boy. You will be nice to him, won't you?

WHITESIDE. God damn it, June, when will you learn that I am *always* kind and courteous! Bring this idiot in!

JUNE. (*Up to door* U.R. *Calling through the dining room, in a low voice.*) Sandy. Sandy.

(*She stands aside as a* YOUNG MAN *enters. Twenty-three or four, keen-looking, neatly but simply dressed.*)

Here he is, Mr. Whiteside. This is Sandy. (*Coming down with* SANDY.)

SANDY. How do you do, sir?

WHITESIDE. How do you do? Young man, I've been hearing a good deal about you from June this past week. It seems, if I have been correctly informed, that you two babes in the woods have quietly gone out of your minds.

JUNE. There's another name for it. It's called love.

WHITESIDE. Well, you've come to the right place. Dr. Sheridan Whiteside, Broken Hearts Mended, Brakes Relined, Hamburgers. Go right ahead.

SANDY. Well, if June has told you anything at all, Mr. Whiteside, you know the jam we're in. You see, I work for the labor union, Mr. Whiteside. I'm an organizer. I've been organizing the men in Mr. Stanley's factory, and Mr. Stanley's pretty sore about it.

WHITESIDE. I'll bet!

SANDY. Did June tell you that?

WHITESIDE. Yes, she did.

SANDY. Well, that being the case, Mr. Whiteside, I don't think I have the right to try to influence June. If she marries me it means a definite break with her family, and I don't like to bring that about. But the trouble is Mr. Stanley's so stubborn about it, so arbitrary. You know, this is not something I've done just to spite him. We fell in love with each other. But Mr. Stanley behaves as though it were all a big plot—John L. Lewis sent me here just to marry his daughter.

JUNE. He's tried to fire Sandy twice, out at the factory, but he couldn't on account of the Wagner Act, thank God!

SANDY. Yes, he thinks I wrote that, too.

JUNE. If he'd only let me talk to him. If he'd let Sandy talk to him.

SANDY. Well, we've gone over all that, June. Anyway, this morning I got word I'm needed in Chicago. I may have to go on to Frisco from there. So you see the jam we're in.

JUNE. Sandy's leaving tonight, Mr. Whiteside. He'll probably be gone a year. We've simply got to decide. *Now.*

WHITESIDE. My dear, this is absurdly simple. It's no problem at all. Now to my jaundiced eye—(*As phone rings. Nods.*) Ohh! Hello . . . Yes . . . This is Whiteside. (*To* JUNE *and* SANDY.) Excuse me—it's a Trans-Atlantic call . . . (*Back to phone.* SANDY *crosses to* L. *of* JUNE.) Yes? . . . Yes, I'm on. Who's calling? . . . Oh! Put him on. (*Again an aside.*) It's Walt Disney in Hollywood. (*Into phone.*) Hello . . . Hello . . . , Walt. How's my little dash of genius? . . . Yes, I hoped you would. How'd you know I was here? . . . I see . . . Yes. Yes, I'm listening. Now? Ten seconds more? (*To* SANDY *and* JUNE.) Mr. Disney calls me every Christmas—(*Into phone again.*) Yes, Walt . . . Yes I hear it. It sounds just like static. . . . June! (*He extends receiver to her; she listens a second, then crosses back to* SANDY C.) Hello . . . Thanks, old

40

man, and a very Merry Christmas to *you* . . . Tell me, is there any news in Hollywood? Who's in Lana Turner's sweater these days? . . . I see . . . Well, goodbye, and don't worry about "Fantasia." It wasn't your fault—Beethoven hasn't written a hit in years . . . Good-bye. (*He hangs up and turns to* JUNE.) Do you know what that was you listened to? The voice of Donald Duck.

JUNE. Not really?

WHITESIDE. Mr. Disney calls me every Christmas, no matter where I am, so that I can hear it. Two years ago I was walking on the bottom of the ocean in a diving-suit, with William Beebe, but he got me . . . Now, where were we? Oh, yes . . . June, I like your young man. I have an unerring instinct about people—I've never been wrong. That's why I wanted to meet him. My feeling is that you two will be very happy together. Whatever his beliefs are, he's entitled to them, and you shouldn't let anything stand in your way. As I see it, it's no problem at all. Stripped of its externals, what does it come down to? Your father. The possibility of making him unhappy. Is that right?

JUNE. *Very* unhappy.

WHITESIDE. That isn't the point. Suppose your parents *are* unhappy —it's good for them. Develops their characters. Look at *me*. I left home at the age of four and haven't been back since. They hear me on the radio and that's enough for them.

SANDY. Then—your advice is to go ahead, Mr. Whiteside?

WHITESIDE. It is. Marry him tonight, June.

JUNE. (*Almost afraid to make the leap.*) You—you mean that, Mr. Whiteside?

WHITESIDE. No, I mean you should marry Hamilton Fish. If I didn't mean it I wouldn't say it. What do you want me to do—say it all over again? My own opinion is you're not worthy of this young man.

STANLEY. (*Upstairs.*) (*Cue:—"say it all over again?"*) Come along, Daisy—stop dawdling.

JUNE. (*Pushing* SANDY *up* R. *and returning to room.* SANDY *exits.*) There's Dad.

STANLEY. (*Descending stairs, and crossing* L. *to coat-rack.*) Forgive us for trespassing, Mr. Whiteside.

WHITESIDE. Not at all, old fellow—not at all. It's Christmas, you know. Merry Christmas, Merry Christmas.

MRS. STANLEY. (*Nervously.*) Ah—yes. Merry Christmas . . . Would you like to come along with us, June? We're taking some presents over to the Dexters'.

JUNE. No—no, thank you, Mother. I—I have to write some letters. *(She goes up stairs.)*

STANLEY. Come along, Daisy.

WHITESIDE. Why, Mr. Stanley, what happened to your forehead? Did you have an accident?

STANLEY. No, Mr. Whiteside. I'm taking boxing lessons. . . . Go ahead, Daisy. *(They go L.)* *(HARRIET, who has been hovering at head of stairs, hurries down as the STANLEYS depart. She is carrying a little Christmas package.)*

HARRIET. *(Crosses R.)* Dear Mr. Whiteside, I've been trying all day to see you. To give you—*this.*

WHITESIDE. Why, Miss Stanley. A Christmas gift for me?

HARRIET. It's only a trifle, but I wanted you to have it. It's a picture of me as I used to be. It was taken on another Christmas Eve, many years ago. Don't open it till the stroke of midnight, *will you?*

(The doorbell rings. HARRIET *looks apprehensively over her shoulder.)* Merry Christmas, dear Mr. Whiteside. Merry Christmas. *(JOHN enters up L. to exit L.)*

WHITESIDE. Merry Christmas to you, Miss Stanley, and thank you. *(She glides out of the room, up R.)* *(In hallway, as JOHN opens door, we hear a woman's voice, liquid and melting: "This is the Stanley residence, isn't it?" "Yes, it is." "I've come to see MR.* WHITESIDE. *Will you tell him MISS SHELDON is here?")* Lorraine! My Blossom Girl!

LORRAINE. *(Coming into view. Enter L. to up L.)* Sherry, my sweet! *(And quite a view it is.* LORRAINE SHELDON *is known as the most chic actress on the New York or London stage, and justly so. She glitters as she walks. She is beautiful, and even, God save the word, glamorous. . . . Her rank as one of the Ten Best Dressed Women of the World is richly deserved. She is, in short, a siren of no mean talents, and knows it.)* *(Crossing R. to him—wasting no time.)* Oh, darling, look at that poor sweet tortured face! Let me kiss it! *(She does.)* You poor darling. How drawn you are. Sherry, my sweet, I want to cry.

WHITESIDE. All right. You've made a very nice entrance, dear. Now relax.

LORRAINE. But, Sherry, darling, I've been so worried. And now seeing you in that chair . . .

WHITESIDE. This chair fits my fanny as nothing else ever has. I feel better than I have in years, and my only concern is news of the out-

42

side world. So take off that skunk and tell me everything. How are you, my dear?

LORRAINE. (*Crossing* L. *to sofa.*) (*Removing a cascade of silver fox from her shoulders.*) Darling, I'm so relieved. You look perfectly wonderful—I never saw you look better. My dear, do I look a wreck? I just dashed through New York. Didn't do a thing about Christmas. Hattie Carnegie and had my hair done, and got right on the train. (*Sits arm of couch. Uses her compact.*) And the Normandie coming back was simply hectic. Fun, you know, but simply exhausting. Jock Whitney, and Cary Grant, and Dorothy di Frasso —it was *too* exhausting. And of course London before that was so magnificent, my dear—well, I simply never got to bed at all. (*Rises. Crosses to* C.) Darling, I've so much to tell you I don't know where to start.

WHITESIDE. Well, start with the dirt first, dear—that's what I want to hear.

LORRAINE. (*Sits on stool.*) Let me see. Sybil Cartwright was thrown right out of Ciro's—it was the night before I left. She was wearing one of those new cellophane dresses, and you could absolutely see Trafalgar Square. And Sir Harry Montross—the painter, you know —is suing his mother for disorderly conduct. It's just shocked *everyone.* And oh! before I forget: Anthony Eden told me he's going to be on your New Year's broadcast, Sherry, and Beatrice Lillie gave me a message for you. She says for you to take off twenty-five pounds right away and send them to her by parcel post. She needs them.

WHITESIDE. I'll pack 'em in ice . . . Now come, dear, what about you? What about your love life? I don't believe for one moment you never got to bed at all, if you'll pardon the expression.

LORRAINE. Sherry dear, you're dreadful.

WHITESIDE. What about that splendid bit of English mutton, Lord Bottomley? Haven't you hooked him yet?

LORRAINE. Sherry, please. Cedric is a very dear friend of mine.

WHITESIDE. Now, Blossom Girl, this is Sherry. Don't try to pull the bedclothes over my eyes. Don't tell *me* you wouldn't like to be Lady Bottomley, with a hundred thousand pounds a year and twelve castles. By the way, has he had his teeth fixed yet? Every time I order Roquefort cheese I think of those teeth.

LORRAINE. Sherry, really! . . . Cedric may not be brilliant, but he's rather sweet, poor lamb, and he's very fond of me, and he does represent a kind of English way of living that I like. Surrey, and

43

London for the season—shooting-box in Scotland—that lovely old castle in Wales. You were there, Sherry—you know what I mean.

WHITESIDE. Mm. I do indeed.

LORRAINE. Well, really, Sherry, why not? If I can marry Cedric, I don't know why I shouldn't. Shall I tell you something, Sherry? I think, from something he said just before I sailed, that he's finally coming around to it. It wasn't definite, mind you, but—don't be surprised if I *am* Lady Bottomley before very long.

WHITESIDE. Lady Bottomley! Won't Kansas City be surprised! However, I shall be a flower-girl and give the groom an iron toothpick as a wedding present. Come ahead, my blossom,—let's hear some more of your skulduggery.

LORRAINE. Well . . .

(*The library doors are quietly opened at this point and the* DOCTOR'S *head appears* D.R.)

BRADLEY. (*In a heavy whisper.*) Mr. Whiteside.

WHITESIDE. What? No, no—not now. I'm busy. (*The* DOCTOR *disappears* D.R., *closes doors.*)

LORRAINE. Who's that?

WHITESIDE. He's fixing the plumbing . . . Now come on, come on—I want some news.

LORRAINE. But, Sherry, what about this play? After all, I've come all the way from New York—even on Christmas Eve—I've been so excited ever since your phone call. Where is it? When can I read it?

WHITESIDE. Well, here's the situation. This young author—his name is Bert Jefferson—brought me the play with the understanding that I send it to Kit Cornell. It's a magnificent part, and God knows I feel disloyal to Kit.

LORRAINE. Sherry.

WHITESIDE. Anyhow, there you are. Now *I've* done *this* much—the rest is up to you. He's young and attractive—now, just how you'll go about persuading him, I'm sure you know more about than I do.

LORRAINE. (*Rises, to* C.) Darling, how can I ever thank you? Does he know I'm coming—Mr. Jefferson, I mean?

WHITESIDE. No, no. You're just out here visiting me. You'll meet him, and that's that. Get him to take you to dinner, and work around to the play. Good God, I don't have to tell you how to do these things. How did you get all those other parts?

LORRAINE. (*Crossing* L. *to sofa for furs and then back.*) Sherry!

44

. . . Well, I'll go back to the hotel and get into something more attractive. I just dumped my bags and rushed right over here. Darling, you're wonderful. (*Lightly kissing him. Crosses to* C.)

WHITESIDE. All right—now run along and get into your working clothes. Then come right back here and spend Christmas Eve with Sherry and I'll have Mr. Jefferson on tap . . . By the way, I've got a little surprise for you. Who do you think's paying me a flying visit tonight? None other than your old friend and co-star, Beverly Carlton.

LORRAINE. (*Crosses to* R. *of couch.*) (*Not too delighted.*) Really? Beverly? I thought he was being glamorous again, on a tramp steamer.

WHITESIDE. Come, come dear—mustn't be bitter because he got better notices than you did.

LORRAINE. Don't be silly, Sherry. I never read notices. I simply wouldn't care to act with him again, that's all. He's not staying here, is he? I hope not.

WHITESIDE. Temper, temper, temper. No, he's not. . . . Where'd you get that diamond clip, dear? That's a new bit of loot, isn't it?

LORRAINE. (*To him.*) Haven't you seen this before? Cedric gave it to me for his mother's birthday. She was simply furious. Look, darling, I've got a taxi outside. *If* I'm *going* to get back here— (*Crossing* L. *to* C.) (*At this point the voice of* MAGGIE *is heard in hallway.*)

MAGGIE. (*Entering* L.) Sherry, what do you think? I've just been given the most beautiful . . . (*She stops short and comes to a dead halt as she sees* LORRAINE.)

LORRAINE. Oh, hello, Maggie. I knew you must be around somewhere. How are you, my dear?

WHITESIDE. (MAGGIE *eases down.*) Santa's been at work, my pet. Blossom Girl just dropped in out of the blue and surprised us.

MAGGIE. (*Up* L., *quietly.*) Hello, Lorraine.

WHITESIDE. (*As* JEFFERSON *appears* L.) Who's that—Bert? Come in, Bert. This is Mr. Bert Jefferson, Lorraine. Young newspaper man. Miss Lorraine Sheldon.

BERT. How do you do, Miss Sheldon?

LORRAINE. How do you do? I didn't quite catch the name—Jefferson?

WHITESIDE. (*Sweetly.*) That's right, Pet.

LORRAINE. (*Crossing up* L.) (MAGGIE *puts coat off and lays it on stool up* L.) (*Full steam ahead.*) Why, Mr. Jefferson, you don't

45

look like a newspaper man. You don't look like a newspaper man at all.

BERT. Really? I thought it was written all over me in Neon lights.

LORRAINE. Oh, no, not at all. I should have said you were—oh, I don't know—an aviator or an explorer or something. They have that same kind of dash about them. I'm simply enchanted with your town, Mr. Jefferson. It gives one such a warm, gracious feeling. Tell me—have you lived here all your life? (*Crosses to* BERT, *up* L.) (MAGGIE *crossing* R. *to up* C.)

BERT. Practically.

WHITESIDE. If you wish to hear the story of his life, Lorraine, kindly do so on your own time. Maggie and I have work to do. Get out of here, Jefferson. On your way, Blossom. On your way.

LORRAINE. He's the world's rudest man, isn't he? Can I drop you, Mr. Jefferson? I'm going down to the—Mansion House, I think it's called.

BERT. Thank you, but I've got my car. Suppose I drop you?

LORRAINE. Oh, would you? That'd be lovely—we'll send the taxi off. See you in a little while, Sherry. 'Bye, Maggie. (*Eases up* L.)

BERT. Good-bye, Maggie. (*He turns to* WHITESIDE.) I'm invited back for dinner, am I not?

WHITESIDE. Yes—yes, you are. At Christmas I always feed the needy. Now please stop oozing out—*get* out.

LORRAINE. Come on, Mr. Jefferson. I want to hear more about this charming little town. (*Starts to go.*) And I want to know a good deal about *you*, too. (*And they are gone. Exit* L.) (*There is a slight but pregnant pause after they go.* MAGGIE *simply stands looking at him, waiting for what may come forth.*)

WHITESIDE. (*As though nothing had happened.*) Now let's see, is there a copy of that broadcast here? How much did you say they wanted out—four minutes?

MAGGIE. (*Eases down* C.) That's right. Four minutes—She's looking very well, isn't she?

WHITESIDE. What's that? Who?

MAGGIE. The Countess di Pushover. Quite a surprise, wasn't it—her dropping in?

WHITESIDE. Yes—yes, it was. Now come on, Maggie, come on. Get to work. Get to work.

MAGGIE. Why, she must have gone through New York like a dose of salts. How long's she going to stay?

WHITESIDE. (*Completely absorbed.*) What? Oh, I don't know—

46

a few days . . . (*He reads from his manuscript.*) "At this joyous season of the year, when in the hearts of men—" I can't cut that.

MAGGIE. Isn't it curious? There was Lorraine, snug as a bug in somebody's bed on the Normandie—

WHITESIDE. (*So busy with his manuscript.*) "Ere the Yuletide season pass—"

MAGGIE. (*Quietly taking manuscript out of his hands.*) (*Crossing* R. *to him, then back to* C.) Now, Sherry dear, we will talk a bit.

WHITESIDE. Now look here, Maggie. Just because a friend of mine happens to come out to spend Christmas with me— (*The door-bell rings.*) I have a hunch that's Beverly. Maggie, see if it is. Go ahead —run! run!

(JOHN *enters up* L. *to exit off* L.) (MAGGIE *looks at him—right through him, in fact. Then she goes slowly toward door* L. "*Magpie*"—*from* BEVERLY. *We hear her voice at the door:* "*Beverly!*" *Then, in clipped English tones:* "*A large, moist, incestuous kiss for my* Magpie!")

(WHITESIDE, *roaring.*) Come in here, you Piccadilly pen-pusher, and gaze upon a soul in agony. (JOHN *exit up* L.) (BEVERLY CARLTON *enters* L., *crosses to* C. *arm in arm with* MAGGIE. *Very confident, very British, very Beverly Carlton. He throws his coat over newel-post,* MAGGIE *puts his hat on table back of couch.*)

BEVERLY. Don't tell me how you are, Sherry dear. I want none of the tiresome details. I have only a little time, so the conversation will be entirely about *me,* and I shall love it. Shall— (*Eases* R.) I tell you how I glittered through the South Seas like a silver scimitar, or would you rather hear how I frolicked through Zambesia, raping the Major-General's daughter and finishing a three-act play at the same time? (*Crosses to* MAGGIE L.) Magpie dear, you are the moon-flower of my middle age, and I love you very much. Say something tender to me.

MAGGIE. Beverly, darling.

BEVERLY. That's my girl. (*Turning to* WHITESIDE.) Now then. Sherry dear, without going into mountainous waves of self-pity, how are you? (*A quick nod of the head.*)

WHITESIDE. I'm fine, you presumptuous Cockney . . . Now, how was the trip, wonderful? (MAGGIE *sits arm of sofa.*)

BEVERLY. (*Crosses* R., *then* U.L.) Fabulous. I did a fantastic amount of work. By the way, did I glimpse that little boudoir butterfly, La Sheldon, in a motor-car as I came up the driveway?

MAGGIE. You did indeed. She's paying us a Christmas visit.

BEVERLY. Dear girl! They do say she set fire to her mother, but I don't believe it . . . Sherry, (*Sits on stool* R.C.) my evil one, not only have I written the finest comedy since Molière, but also the best revue since my last one, and an operetta that frightens me it's so good. I shall play it for eight weeks in London and six in New York—that's all. No matinees. Then I am off to the Grecian Islands . . . Magpie, why don't you come along? Why don't you desert this cannon-ball of fluff and come with me?

MAGGIE. Beverly dear, be careful. You're catching me at a good moment.

WHITESIDE. (*Changing the subject.*) Tell me, Beverly, did you have a good time in Hollywood? How long were you there?

BEVERLY. (*Rises, crosses to* C.) Three unbelievable days. I saw everyone from Adrian to Zanuck. They came, poor dears, as to a shrine. I was insufferably charming and ruthlessly firm in refusing seven million dollars for two minutes' work.

WHITESIDE. What about Banjo? Did you see my wonderful Banjo in Hollywood?

BEVERLY. I did. He gave a dinner for me. I arrived, in white tie and tails to be met at the door by two bewigged butlers, who quietly proceeded to take my trousers off. I was then ushered, in my lemon silk drawers, into a room full of Norma Shearer, Claudette Colbert, and Aldous Huxley, among others. Dear, sweet, incomparable Banjo. (*Crossing to couch, he puts his arm about* MAGGIE'S *shoulder.*)

WHITESIDE. I'll never forget that summer at Antibes, when Banjo put a microphone in Lorraine's mattress, and then played the record the next day at lunch.

BEVERLY. (*Crossing* C.) I remember it indeed. Lorraine left Antibes by the next boat.

MAGGIE. (*Half to herself.*) I wish Banjo were here now.

BEVERLY. (*Back to* MAGGIE.) What's the matter, Magpie? Is Lorraine being her own sweet sick-making self?

MAGGIE. You wouldn't take her to the Grecian Islands with you, would you, Beverly? Just for me?

WHITESIDE. Now, now. Lorraine is a charming person who has gallantly given up her own Christmas to spend it with me.

BEVERLY. (*Crosses to* C.) Oh, I knew I had a bit of dirt for us all to nibble on. (*He draws a letter out of his pocket.*) (*Again library doors are opened and the* DOCTOR'S *head comes through,* D.R.)

BRADLEY. Mr. Whiteside.

WHITESIDE. No, no, not now. Go away.

(DOCTOR *withdraws* D.R., *closing doors.*)

BEVERLY. Have you kidnapped someone, Sherry?

WHITESIDE. Yes, that was Charley Ross . . . Go ahead. Is this something juicy?

BEVERLY. (*To stool* L. *of wheelchair—sits.*) Juicy as a pomegranate. It is the latest report from London on the winter manoeuvres of Miss Lorraine Sheldon against the left flank—in fact, all flanks—of Lord Cedric Bottomley. Listen: "Lorraine has just left us in a cloud of Chanel Number Five. Since September, in her relentless pursuit of His Lordship, she has paused only to change girdles and check her oil. She has chased him, panting, from castle to castle, till he finally took refuge, for several week-ends, in the gentlemen's lavatory of the House of Lords. Practically no one is betting on the Derby this year; we are all making book on Lorraine. She is sailing tomorrow on the Normandie, but would return on the Atlantic Clipper if Bottomley so much as belches in her direction." Have you ever met Lord Bottomley, Magpie dear? (*Rise to* C.)

MAGGIE. No, I haven't. (HE *goes immediately into an impersonation of His Lordship. Very British, very full of teeth, stuttering.*) "Not v-v-very good shooting today, blast it. Only s-s-six partridges, f-f-four grouse and the D-D-Duke of Sutherland. Haw, haw."

WHITESIDE. (*Chuckling.*) My God, that's Bottomley to his very bottom.

BEVERLY. (*Still in character.*) "R-r-ripping debate in the House today. Old Basil spoke for th-th-three hours. D-d-dropped dead at the end of it. Ripping. Haw!" (*Eases* L.)

MAGGIE. You're making it up, Beverly. No one sounds like that.

WHITESIDE. It's so good it's uncanny . . . Damn it, Beverly, why must you race right out of here? I never see enough of you, you ungrateful moppet.

BEVERLY. (*Crosses* R. *to* WHITESIDE.) Sherry darling, I can only tell you that my love for you is so great that I changed trains at Chicago to spend ten minutes with you and wish you a Merry Christmas. Merry Christmas, my lad. My little Magpie. (MAGGIE *rises to* C.)

MAGGIE. Beverly!

BEVERLY. (*A look at his watch, crosses* L. *to piano* D.L.) And now I have just time for one magnificent number, to give you a taste of how brilliant the whole thing is. It's the second number from my new revue. (*He strikes chord on piano, but before he can go further the phone rings.*)

WHITESIDE. Oh, damn! Get rid of them, Maggie. (MAGGIE *crosses to phone* D.R. *on large ottoman* R. *of wheelchair.* MAGGIE, *whose mind is on other things, abstractedly reaches for phone.*)

MAGGIE. Hello . . . Oh, hello, Bert. Oh! Well, just a minute. Beverly, would you talk to a newspaper man for just two minutes? I kind of promised him.

BEVERLY. (*During phone conversation, softly playing a few bars of a "former" hit.*) Won't have time, Magpie, unless he's under the piano.

MAGGIE. Oh! (*Into phone.*) Wait a minute. (*To* BEVERLY *again.*) Would you see him at the station, just for a minute before the train goes? (BEVERLY *nods.*) Bert, go to the station and wait for him. He'll be there in a few minutes . . . 'Bye.

WHITESIDE. The stalls are impatient, Beverly. Let's have this second-rate masterpiece. (MAGGIE *at stool* R.C.)

BEVERLY. (*His fingers rippling over the keys.*) It's called: "What Am I To Do?"[1]

"Oft in the nightfall
   I think I might fall
   Down from my perilous height;
Deep in the heart of me,
Always a part of me,
   Quivering, shivering light.
Run, little lady,
Ere the shady
   Shafts of time,
Barb you with their winged desire,
Singe you with their sultry fire.
   Softly a fluid
             Druid
                Meets me,

"Olden
   and golden
      the dawn that greets me;
Cherishing,
   So perishing,
Up to the stars
   I climb.

1. For music see page 82.

"What am I to do toward
Ending this madness,
This sadness
That's rending me through?
The flowers of yesteryear are haunting me,
Taunting me,
Darling, for wanting you.

"What am I to say
To warnings of sorrow,
When warning's tomorrow drinks the dew?
Will I see the cosmic Ritz
Shattered and scattered to bits.
What not am I to do?"

MAGGIE. (*Rising and crossing* L.) Wonderful, Beverly. (BEVERLY
starts to play second chorus.)
WHITESIDE. Beverly, it's *superb*. The best thing you've *ever written*.
(*The doorbell rings and* JOHN *is glimpsed* U.L. *as he goes through
door. It is a trio of* RADIO MEN *who appear in doorway, their arms
filled with equipment for* WHITESIDE'S *broadcast.*)
BEVERLY. Please, let me say that.
WHITESIDE. Ah. Come in, Westcott.
BEVERLY. (*Rise to* D.L. *of piano.*) Ah. The airwaves, eh! Well, I
shan't have to hear you, thank God. I shall be on a train. (WESTCOTT
goes to library D.R., *first handing a microphone to a second* RADIO
MAN, *also carrying a mike. A third man carries a portable control
board.*)
MAGGIE. (*Crossing* D.R.) Mr. Westcott, will you go in that room?
John, will you show them where to plug in? Come on, Whiteside,
say good-bye.
JOHN. Right this way, gentlemen. (THEY *follow him off to dining-
room* U.R.)
WHITESIDE. (*As* MAGGIE *starts to wheel him into library.*) Stop
this nonsense.
BEVERLY. (*Calling after the fast disappearing* WHITESIDE.) Au
revoir, Sherry, Merry Christmas.
WHITESIDE. Beverly, my lamb—Maggie, what the hell are you—I
want to talk to Beverly.
MAGGIE. You can kiss Beverly in London on July twelfth.
WHITESIDE. (*As he is pushed through library door in his wheelchair.*) I won't be rushed out of this room like a baby that has to

51

have his diapers changed. (*He is gone.*)

BEVERLY. (*Gathering up his hat and coat.*) Magpie, come get a kiss.

MAGGIE. (*Crossing up* L.) (*Emerging from library and closing doors behind her.*) Beverly, I want one minute. I must have it. You'll make the train. The station's a minute and a half from here. (BRADLEY *enters* D.R.)

BEVERLY. Why, what's the matter, Magpie? (*At which the library doors are opened and* DOCTOR *emerges rather apologetically.*)

WHITESIDE. (*Offstage.*) Go away!

DOCTOR. I'm—I'm just waiting in the kitchen until Mr.—excuse me. (*He darts out through dining-room. Exits up* R.)·

BEVERLY. (*Back of sofa.*) Who *is* that man?

MAGGIE. Never mind . . . Beverly, I'm in great trouble.

BEVERLY. Magpie, dear, what is it?

MAGGIE. I've fallen in love.

BEVERLY. No! (*Taking her hands.*)

MAGGIE. Yes. For the first time in my life. Beverly, I'm in love. I can't tell you about it—there isn't time. But Sherry is trying to break it up. In his own fiendish way he's doing everything he can to break it up.

BEVERLY. Why, the old flounder! What's he doing?

MAGGIE. Lorraine. He's brought Lorraine here to smash it up.

BEVERLY. Oh, it's somebody *here?* In this town?

MAGGIE. (*Nodding.*) He's a newspaper man—the one you're going to see at the station—and he's written a play, and I know Sherry must be using that as bait. You *know* Lorraine—she'll eat him up alive. You've got to help me, Beverly.

BEVERLY. Of course I will, Magpie. What do you want me to do?

MAGGIE. I've got to get Lorraine out of here—the further away the better—and you can do it for me. (WESTCOTT *opens library doors.*)

BEVERLY. But how? How can I? I'm leaving. (*The library doors are opened, and* WESTCOTT *emerges.*)

WESTCOTT: Have you a carbon of the broadcast, Miss Cutler?

MAGGIE. There's one on that table.

WESTCOTT. Thank you. One of those penguins *ate* the original. (*Exit* D.R., *closing doors.*)

MAGGIE. (*Crossing* L. *of* BEVERLY.) (*She lowers her voice.*) Here's what I want you to do. (*Manoeuvring him into hall up* L. *We see her whisper to him; his head bobs up and down quickly in assent. Then he lets out a shriek of laughter.*)

BEVERLY. I'd love it. I'd absolutely love it. (MAGGIE *puts a quick finger to his lips; peers toward the* WHITESIDE *room. But* WESTCOTT *has gone in; doors are closed.*) It's simply enchanting, and bitches Sherry and Lorraine at the same time. It's pure heaven! I adore it, and I shall do it up brown. (*He embraces her.*)

MAGGIE. Darling, the first baby will be named Beverly. You're wonderful.

BEVERLY. Of course I am. Come to Chislewick for your honeymoon and I'll put you up. Goodbye, my lovely. I adore you. (*Sees time on his wrist-watch.*) Mercy! Let me out of here! (*He is gone,* L.) (MAGGIE *comes back into room, highly pleased with herself. She even sings a fragment of* BEVERLY'S *song, "What Am I To Do?" "Tra-la-la-la-la-la."*) (JOHN *entering from dining-room, up* R., *breaks the song.*)

JOHN. (*Crosses down, puts stool up* R. *of tree.*) Shall I straighten up the room for the broadcast, Miss Cutler?

MAGGIE. (*Crosses to* C.) No, John, it isn't television, thank God, they only hear the liquid voice.

JOHN. He's really wonderful, isn't he, Mr. Whiteside? The things he finds time to do.

MAGGIE. (*Crossing* R.) Yes, he certainly sticks his nose into everything, John.

WESTCOTT. (*Enters from library* D.R.) Are the boys out there, Miss Cutler?

MAGGIE. (*As she exits into library, closing doors.*) Yes, they are, Mr. Westcott.

WESTCOTT. (*As he goes into dining-room up* R.) Thank you.

(JOHN *crosses to table* L., *putting room in order as he closes a cigarette box on piano* D.L. *Suddenly* JUNE *comes quietly down stairs. She is dressed for the street and is carrying a suitcase.*)

JOHN. (*At down-stage side piano.*) Why, Miss June, are you going away?

JUNE. (R. *of staircase.*) Why—no, John. No—Mr. Whiteside is in there, I suppose?

JOHN. Yes, he's getting ready to go on the radio.

JUNE. Oh! Would you—no, never mind. Look, John—(*Just then* RICHARD *comes downstairs carrying a light bag and a couple of cameras.*)

RICHARD. Where is he? In the library?

JUNE. Yes, he's busy.

RICHARD. Oh! Well, maybe we ought to—(*Door-bell rings again.*)

Come on. (RICHARD *immediately scoots out, also via dining-room up* R., *shooing* JUNE *before him.* JOHN *meanwhile has gone to front door off* L.)

LORRAINE. Thank you, John. (*It is* LORRAINE *who comes in, resplendent now in evening dress and wrap, straight from Paris. At same time* MAGGIE *emerges from library* D.R. *and* JOHN *goes on his way up* L. MAGGIE *puts the phone back on console* D.R.) (LORRAINE *to* C.) Hello, dear. Where's Sherry?

MAGGIE. Inside working—he's broadcasting very soon. (MAGGIE *puts present from ottoman under tree* U.C.)

LORRAINE. (*Surveying the room.*) Oh, of course—Christmas Eve. What a wonderful man Sheridan Whiteside is. You know, my dear, it must be such an utter joy to be secretary to somebody like Sherry.

MAGGIE. Yes, you meet such interesting people . . . (LORRAINE *crosses to couch.*) That's quite a gown, Lorraine. Going anywhere? (*Chair* D.R.)

LORRAINE. This? Oh, I just threw on anything at all. (*Sits on sofa.*) Aren't you dressing for dinner?

MAGGIE. (*Crosses to back of sofa.*) No, just what meets the eye. (*She has occasion to carry a few papers across room at this point.* LORRAINE'S *eyes watch her narrowly. As* MAGGIE *reaches* C. *she gives* LORRAINE *a polite social smile, then continues to* D.R.)

LORRAINE. Who does your hair, Maggie?

MAGGIE. A little Frenchwoman named Maggie Cutler comes in every morning.

LORRAINE. You know, every time I see you I keep thinking your hair could be so lovely. I always wanted to get my hands on it.

MAGGIE. (*Sits; quietly.*) I've always wanted to get mine on yours, Lorraine.

LORRAINE. (*Absently.*) What, dear? (*One of the* RADIO MEN *drifts into room with a table for control board, puts it* L. *of tree, drifts out again. As he reaches arch* U.R. *he grins broadly.* LORRAINE'S *eyes follow him idly. Then she turns to* MAGGIE *again.*) By the way, what time does Beverly get here? I'm not over-anxious to meet him.

MAGGIE. He's been and gone, Lorraine.

LORRAINE. Really? Well, I'm very glad . . . Of course, you're great friends, aren't you—you and Beverly?

MAGGIE. Yes, we are. I think he's a wonderful person.

LORRAINE. Oh, I suppose he is. But really, when I finished acting with him, I was a perfect wreck. All during that tender love scene

that the critics thought was so magnificent, he kept dropping pea-
nut shells down my dress. I wouldn't act with him again if I were
starving.

MAGGIE. (*Rise, crosses to* C.) Tell me, Lorraine, have you found a
new play yet?

LORRAINE. (*At once on guard.*) No—no, I haven't. There was a
pile of manuscripts waiting in New York for me, but I hurried
right out here to Sherry.

MAGGIE. Yes, it was wonderful of you, Lorraine—to drop everything that way and rush to Sherry's wheel-chair.

LORRAINE. Well, after all, Maggie, dear, what else has one in this
world but friends? . . .

MAGGIE. (*Crosses* R. *to* D.R.) That's what I always say . . . (RADIO
MAN *enters up* R. *with control board, puts it on table.*) Everything
O.K.?

RADIO MAN. Yes, thank you. (*Starting off, never taking his eyes off*
LORRAINE. *He reaches library doors, realizes his mistake, exits into
dining-room* U.R.)

LORRAINE. How long will Sherry be in there?

MAGGIE. (*Crosses to* C.) Not long . . . Did you know that Mr.
Jefferson has written quite a good play? The young man that drove
you to the hotel.

LORRAINE. Really? No, I didn't. Isn't that interesting?

MAGGIE. (*Sits.*) Yes, isn't it?

(*Considerable pause. The ladies smile at each other.*)

LORRAINE. (*Evading* MAGGIE'S *eyes.*) They've put a polish on my
nails I simply loathe. I don't suppose Elizabeth Arden has a branch
in this town.

MAGGIE. (*Busy with her papers.*) Not if she has any sense.

LORRAINE. (*Rises, to back of sofa, then to piano.*) Oh, well, I'll
just bear it, but it does depress me. (*She wanders aimlessly for a
moment. Picks up a book from table.*) Have you read this, Maggie,
everybody was reading it on the boat. I hear you simply can't put it
down.

MAGGIE. *I* put it down—*right there.* (LORRAINE *casually strikes a
note or two on piano.*) (*The phone rings.*) (*Taking up receiver a
little too casually.*) Hello . . . yes . . . Yes . . . Miss Lorraine
Sheldon? Yes, she's here . . . There's a Trans-Atlantic call coming
(*Rises.*) through for you, Lorraine.

LORRAINE. (*Crossing* R. *to phone.*) Trans-Atlantic—for me?
Here? Why, what in the world—

MAGGIE. (*As she hands over receiver—eases up* C.) It's London.

LORRAINE. London? . . . Hello. (*Then in a louder tone.*) Hello . . . Cedric! Cedric, is this you? . . . Why, Cedric, you darling! Why, what a surprise! How'd you know I was here? What . . . ? Darling, don't talk so fast and you won't stutter so . . . That's better . . . Yes, now, I can hear you . . . Yes, very clearly. It's as though you were just around the corner . . . I see . . . What? . . . Darling! (*Realizing* MAGGIE *is listening.*) Cedric, dearest, would you wait just one moment? (*She turns to* MAGGIE.) Maggie, would you mind? It's Lord Bottomley—a *very* personal call. Would you mind?

MAGGIE. Oh, not at all. (*She goes into dining-room, up* R., *almost does a little waltz step as she goes.*)

LORRAINE. Yes, my dearest—now tell me . . . Cedric, please don't stutter so. Don't be nervous. (*She listens for a moment again.*) Oh, my darling. Oh, my sweet. You don't know how I've prayed for this, every night on the boat . . . Darling, yes! YES, a thousand times Yes! . . . I'll take a plane right out of here and catch the next boat . . . What? Cedric, don't stutter so . . . Yes, and I love *you*, my darling—oh, so much! . . . Oh, my dear sweet. My darlingest darling. Yes, yes! I will, I will, darling! I'll be thinking of you every moment . . . You've made me the happiest girl in the world . . . Good-bye, good-bye, darling. Goodbye. (*Puts phone on ottoman* D.R.) (*Bursting with her news, she turns to library to call* WHITESIDE, *opens doors, crosses to* C.) Sherry! Sherry, Sherry! Do you know what happened? Cedric just called from London—he's asked me to marry him.

WHITESIDE. (*Wheeling himself on. He is smoking a cigarette in a long holder.*) What!

LORRAINE. Sherry, think of it! At last! I've got to get right out of here and catch the next boat.

MAGGIE. (*Emerging, mouse-like, from dining-room, up* R.) May I come in?

LORRAINE. (*Crossing* L.) Maggie, dear, can I get a plane out of here right away? I've simply got to get the next boat to England. When is it—do you know? Is there a newspaper here?

MAGGIE. (*Eases down.*) The Queen Mary sails Friday. What's happened?

LORRAINE. (*Crossing up* R., *embraces* MAGGIE.) Maggie, the most wonderful thing in the world has happened. Lord Bottomley has asked me to marry him. Oh, Maggie! (*A gesture toward phone.*)

MAGGIE. Really? Well, what do you know?

LORRAINE. Isn't it wonderful? I'm so excited I can hardly think. Maggie dear, you must help me to get right out of here.

MAGGIE. (*Crossing to desk* D.R.) I'd be delighted to, Lorraine.

LORRAINE. Oh, thank you, thank you. Will you look things up right away?

MAGGIE. Yes, I've a time-table right here. And don't worry, because if there's no train I'll drive you to Cleveland and you can catch the plane from there.

LORRAINE. Maggie darling, you're wonderful. (*She sees* WHITESIDE *puffing furiously on his cigarette.*) Sherry, what's the matter with you? You haven't said a word. You haven't even congratulated me.

WHITESIDE. (*Rolls down* R.) (*He has been sitting through this like a thunder-cloud.*) Let me understand this, Lorraine. Am I to gather from your girlish squeals that you are about to toss your career into the ashcan?

LORRAINE. (*To sofa for furs.*) Oh, not at all. Of course I may not be able to play this season, but there'll be other seasons, Sherry.

WHITESIDE. I see. And everything goes into the ashcan with it—is that right?

LORRAINE. But Sherry, you couldn't expect me to—

WHITESIDE. (*Icily.*) Don't explain, Lorraine. I understand only too well. And I also understand why Cornell remains the First Actress of our theatre.

MAGGIE. (*Busy with her time-tables, crossing to* C.) Oh, this is wonderful! We're in luck, Lorraine. There's a plane out of Cleveland at ten-three. It takes about an hour to get there.—Why it all works out wonderfully, doesn't it, Sherry?

WHITESIDE. (*Through his teeth.*) Peachy.

LORRAINE. (*Heading for phone, crossing* R. *below phone stool* D.R.) Maggie, what's the number of that hotel I'm at? I've got to get my maid started packing.

MAGGIE. Mesalia three-two.

LORRAINE. (*Into phone.*) Mesalia three-two, please . . . Let's see —I sail Friday, five-day boat, that means I ought to be in London Wednesday night . . . (MAGGIE *crosses up* L.) Hello, this is Miss Sheldon . . . That's right. Put me through to my maid, will you?

MAGGIE. (*At window.*) Oh, look, Sherry, it's starting to snow. Isn't that wonderful, Sherry? Oh, I never felt more like Christmas in my life. Don't you, Sherry dear?

WHITESIDE. Shut your nasty little face! (MAGGIE *drifts down* L. *and*

57

leans against piano.)

LORRAINE. (*On phone. She sits on ottoman* D.R.) Cosette? . . . Now listen carefully, Cosette. We're leaving here tonight by plane and sailing Friday on the Queen Mary. I want you to start packing immediately and I'll call for you in about an hour . . . Yes, that's right . . . Now I want you to send these cables for me. Have you got a pencil? Right? The first one goes to Lord and Lady Cunard— you'll find all these addresses in my little book. It's in my dressing case. "Lord and Lady Cunard. My darlings. Returning Friday Queen Mary. Cedric and I being married immediately on arrival. Wanted you to be the first to know. Love—Lorraine." Now send— what? Oh, thank you, Cosette. Thank you very much. (*This last "thank you" followed by a pointed smile at Sherry.*) Now send the same message to Lady Astor, Lord Beaverbrook, and my mother in Kansas City . . . got that? And send a telegram to Hattie Carnegie, New York. "Please meet me Sherry Netherlands noon tomorrow with sketches of bridal gown and trousseau.—Lorraine Sheldon." And then send one to Monsieur Pierre Cartier, Cartier's, London: "Will you hold in reserve for me the triple string of pearls I picked out in October? Cable me Queen Mary.—Lorraine Sheldon." Have you got all that straight, Cosette? . . . That's fine. Now you'll have to rush, my dear—I'll be at the hotel in about an hour, so be ready. Good-bye. (*She hangs up, putting phone on ottoman. She crosses back of Sherry's chair to* C.) Thank goodness for Cosette—I'd die without her, she's the most wonderful maid in the world . . . Well! Life is really just full of surprises, isn't it? Who'd have thought an hour ago that I'd be on my way to London?

MAGGIE. An *hour* ago? No, I certainly wouldn't have thought it an hour ago.

WHITESIDE. (*Beside himself with temper.*) Will you both stop this female drooling? I have a violent headache.

MAGGIE. (*All solicitude. Crossing* R. *front sofa.*) Oh, Sherry! Can I get you something?

LORRAINE. (*Crossing to Sherry.*) Look here, Sherry, I'm sorry if I've offended you, but after all my life is my own and—(*She stops as* BERT *comes in from outside.*)

BERT. (*To* C.) Hello, everybody. Say, do you know it's snowing out? Going to have a real old-fashioned Christmas.

WHITESIDE. Why don't you telephone your scoop to the New York Times?

MAGGIE. (*Crosses to him.*) Bert, Miss Sheldon has to catch a plane tonight, from Cleveland. Can we drive her over, you and I?

BERT. Why, certainly. Sorry you have to go, Miss Sheldon. No bad news, I hope.

LORRAINE. Oh, on the contrary—very good news. Wonderful news.

MAGGIE. Yes, indeed—calls for a drink, I think. You're not being a very good host, Sherry. How about a bottle of champagne? (*Crossing* R.)

BERT. Oh, I can do better than that—let me mix you a Jefferson Special. Okay, Mr. Whiteside?

WHITESIDE. Yes, yes, yes, yes, yes. Mix anything. Only stop drivelling.

BERT. Anybody admired my Christmas present yet, Maggie?

MAGGIE. Oh, dear, I forgot. (*She raises her arm, revealing a bracelet.*) Look everybody! From Mr. Jefferson to me.

LORRAINE. Oh, it's charming. Let me see it. Oh! Why, it's inscribed, too. "To Maggie. Long may she wave. Bert." Maggie, it's a lovely Christmas present. Isn't that sweet, Sherry?

WHITESIDE. Ducky.

MAGGIE. (*Crosses to* L.C.) I told you it was beautiful, Bert. See?

BERT. Well, shows what you get if you save your coupons.

LORRAINE. (*Looking from* BERT *to* MAGGIE.) Well, what's going on between you two, anyhow? Maggie, are you hiding something from us?

WHITESIDE. (*A hand to his head.*) Great God, will this drivel never stop? My head is bursting.

BERT. (*Crosses up* R., *then back to* WHITESIDE.) A Jefferson Special will cure anything . . . By the way, I got a two-minute interview with Beverly Carlton at the station. You were right, Mr. Whiteside—he's quite something. (LORRAINE *crosses up* L. *and drifts down to piano.*)

MAGGIE. (*Uneasily.*) Go ahead, Bert—mix the drinks.

BERT. On the fire. I was lucky to get even two minutes. He was in a telephone booth most of the time. (*Light slowly starts to dawn on* WHITESIDE.)

MAGGIE. Bert, mix those drinks, will you?

BERT. Okay, couldn't hear what he was saying, but from the faces he was making, it looked like a scene from one of his plays.

MAGGIE. Bert, for goodness' sake, will you—

WHITESIDE. (*Suddenly galvanized.*) Ah—just a minute, if you please, Jefferson. Mr. Carlton was in a telephone booth at the station?

BERT. (*Coming* D.R.) Certainly was—I thought he'd never come out. Kept talking and making the damnedest faces for about five minutes.

WHITESIDE. (*Ever so sweetly.*) Bert, my boy, I have an idea I shall love the Jefferson Special. Make me a double one, will you? My headache has gone with the wind.

BERT. Okay. (*He goes up* R.)

WHITESIDE. (*His eyes gleaming, immediately grabs phone.*) Philo Vance is now at work. Hello. (MAGGIE *eases* L. *to piano front.*) (*On phone—his voice is absolutely musical.*) Operator dear, has there been a call from England over this telephone within the past half hour . . . ? (LORRAINE *eases* R.) Yes, I'll wait.

LORRAINE. (*Eases* R.) Sherry, what *is* all this?

WHITESIDE. Sssh!—What's that? There have been no calls from England for the past three days? Thank you . . . Blossom Girl. (*She crosses to hi*r.) Now, will you repeat that, please? (*He beckons to* LORRAINE, *then puts receiver to her ear.*) Hear it, dear? (*Then again to operator.*) Thank you, operator, and a Merry Christmas. (*He hangs up.*)

LORRAINE. (*Stunned.*) Sherry, what is all this? What does this mean?

WHITESIDE. My dear, you have just played the greatest love-scene of your career with your old friend Beverly Carlton.

LORRAINE. Why—why, that's not true. I was talking to Cedric. What do you mean?

WHITESIDE. I mean, my blossom, that that was Beverly you poured out your girlish heart to, not Lord Bottomley. Ah, me, who'd have thought five minutes ago that you would not be going to London!

LORRAINE. Sherry, I want this explained.

WHITESIDE. Explained? You heard the operator, my dear. All I can tell you is that Beverly was indulging in one of his famous bits of mimicry, that's all. You've heard him do Lord Bottomley before, haven't you?

LORRAINE. Yes . . . Yes, of course . . . But—but why would he want to do such a thing? This is one of the most dreadful—oh, my God! Those cables! Those cables! (*In one bound she crosses back of wheelchair, to phone.*) Give me the hotel—whatever it's called— I want the hotel . . . I'll pay him off for this if it's the last thing that I—why, the skunk!—the louse! The dirty rotten—Mansion House? Connect me with the maid . . . What? . . . Who the hell do you *think* it is? Miss Sheldon, of course . . . Oh! God! Those cables. If only Cosette hasn't—Cosette! Cosette! Did you send those cables? . . . Oh, God! Oh, God! . . . Now listen, Cosette, I want you to send another cable to every one of those people, and tell them somebody has been using my name, and to disregard anything and everything they hear from me—except this, of course . . . Don't ask questions—do as you're told . . . Don't argue with me, you French bitch—God damn it, do as you're told . . . And unpack, we're not going! (*She hangs up and crosses* U.L.)

WHITESIDE. Now steady, my blossom. Take it easy.

LORRAINE. (*Crossing back to* C.) What do you mean take it easy? Do you realize I'll be the laughing stock of England? Why, I won't dare show my face! I always knew Beverly Carlton was low, but not this low. Why? WHY? It isn't even funny. Why would he do it, that's what I'd like to know. Why would he do it! Why would anyone in the world want to play a silly trick like this? I can't understand it. Do you, Sherry? Do you, Maggie? You both saw him this afternoon. Why would he walk out of here, (*Crosses to* MAGGIE, *then back to* C.) go right to a phone booth, and try to ship me over to England on a fool's errand! There must have been some reason—there must have. It doesn't make sense otherwise. Why would Beverly Carlton, or anybody else for that matter, want me to—? (*She stops as a dim light begins to dawn.*)

(MAGGIE *hand to hair.*) Oh! Oh! (*Her eye, which has been on* MAGGIE, *goes momentarily to dining-room, where* BERT *has disappeared. Then her gaze returns to* MAGGIE *again.*) I—I think I begin to—of course! Of course! That's it. Of course that's it. Yes, and that's a very charming bracelet that Mr. Jefferson gave you—isn't it, Maggie, dear? Of course. It makes complete sense now. And to think that I nearly—well! Wild horses couldn't get me out of here now, (*Crossing to* MAGGIE L.) Maggie, and if I were you I'd hang onto that bracelet, dear. It'll be something to remember him by. (*Crosses to front of sofa.*) (*Out of dining-room comes* WESTCOTT, *his hands full of papers. At same time the two* TECHNICIANS *emerge, 1st man goes to control board, the other sets two standing mikes* D.C. *and* L.C. *of wheelchair.*)

WESTCOTT. (*His eyes on his watch. Crosses to* R. *of wheelchair.*) All right, Mr. Whiteside. Almost time. Hook her up boys, start testing. Here's your new copy, Mr. Whiteside. (*Hands typed copy to him.*)

WHITESIDE. How much time?

WESTCOTT. Couple of minutes.

(IST RADIO MAN *is talking into his control board apparatus, testing,* "One, two, three, four, one, two, three, four. How are we coming in, New York? . . . A, B, C, D, A, B, C, D. Mary had a little lamb, Mary had a little lamb.")

(MR. *and* MRS. STANLEY, *having delivered their Christmas presents, enter from hallway* L. STANLEY *stops to take his coat off.* MRS. STANLEY *looks hungrily at radio goings-on. The voice of* 2ND RADIO MAN *drones on:* "Testing." *But* STANLEY *delivers a stern* "Please, Daisy," *and she follows him up stairs.* "O.K. New York. Mary had a little lamb. Waiting." WESTCOTT *stands with watch in hand. From dining-room comes* BERT, *tray of four drinks in hand.*)

BERT. (*Crosses to* C.) Here comes the Jefferson Special . . . Oh! Have we time?

LORRAINE. (*Below couch* L.) Oh, I'm sure we have. Mr. Jefferson, I'm not leaving after all. My plans are changed.

BERT. (*Crosses* L.) Really? Oh, that's good.

LORRAINE. And I hear you've written a simply marvelous play, Mr. Jefferson. I want you to read it to me—tonight. Will you? We'll go back to the Mansion House right after dinner. And you'll read me your play. (*She takes a cocktail.*) (MAGGIE *steps downstage.*)

BERT. Why—why, I should say so. I'd be delighted . . . Maggie, did you hear that? (*Crosses* L. *to* D.L.) Say, I'll bet *you* did this. You arranged the whole thing. Well, it's the finest Christmas present you could have given me. (MAGGIE *looks at him for one anguished moment. Then, without a word, she dashes into hall,* L., *grabs her coat and flings herself out of the house.*) Maggie! Maggie! (BERT *puts tray of drinks on piano and starts after her, but stops when he hears door slam.* LORRAINE, *meanwhile, sits on sofa.*)

FIRST RADIO MAN. Thirty seconds. Waiting. (MR. *and* MRS. STANLEY *come pell-mell down stairs. Each clutches a letter and they are wild-eyed.*)

STANLEY. (C.) Mr. Whiteside!

WESTCOTT. Quiet, please!

STANLEY. My son has run off on a freighter, and my daughter is marrying an Anarchist.

WESTCOTT. Quiet!

STANLEY. They say you told them to do it.

MRS. STANLEY. My poor June! My poor Richard! This is the most awful—

WESTCOTT. Quiet! Quiet, please! We're going on the air.

(*Enter* CHOIR BOYS L., *cross to* C.) (STANLEY *chokes and looks bewilderedly at the letter in his hand.* MRS. STANLEY *is softly crying.*)

(DR. BRADLEY *emerges from dining-room.*)

BRADLEY. Oh! I see you're still busy.

STANLEY. Don't tell me to be quiet!

WESTCOTT. (*Yelling, he pushes* STANLEYS *upstage.*) Quiet! For God's sake, quiet! Step out of the way. Please! All right, boys, right this way. Down here to this mike. (*Crosses* L. *to usher* BOYS *to* C. *mike.*) (*From hallway come six* CHOIR BOYS *dressed in their robes. They take their places by the microphone. The moment they are set, one of the boys blows pitch-pipe for key.*)

IST RADIO MAN. (*Completing hookup.*) O.K. New York.

(2ND RADIO MAN *raises his arm when* CHOIR BOYS *are set.* WEST-COTT *is watching him. A dead pause of about five seconds.* JOHN *and* SARAH *are on tip-toe in dining-room. Then the arm drops.* WESTCOTT *gestures to* CHOIR BOYS *to sing. They raise their lovely voices in "Silent Night.")*

WESTCOTT. (*Into microphone* C.) Good evening, everybody. Cream of Mush brings you Sheridan Whiteside. (WESTCOTT, *lowering mike, gestures to* CHOIR BOYS *to step forward to mike. Another gesture from* WESTCOTT, *who has crossed to* R. *of chair, and* WHITE-SIDE *begins to speak, with* BOYS *singing as a background.*)

CHOIR BOYS. (*Singing, "Silent Night."*)

Silent night, holy night,

All is calm, all is bright

Round yon Virgin Mother and Child.

Holy infant so tender and mild,

Sleep in heavenly peace,

Sleep in heavenly peace.

(WESTCOTT *crosses* D.R.)

WHITESIDE. (*Simultaneously.*) This is Whiteside speaking. On this eve of eves, when my own heart is overflowing with peace and kindness, I think it most fitting to tell once again the story of that still and lustrous night, nigh onto two thousand years ago—

(*At this point there is a piercing scream from library* D.R. *Everybody turns at interruption as* MISS PREEN *rushes on, holding her hand. The choir continues to sing during all of this.*)

MISS PREEN. A penguin bit me! (BRADLEY *crosses to her.*)

WHITESIDE. (*Raising his voice to top the sobbing* MISS PREEN, *continues.*) When first the star of Bethlehem—(*The curtain starts down.*) was glimpsed in a wondrous sky . . .

THE CURTAIN IS DOWN
(Medium)

ACT THREE

Scene is the same.

Christmas morning. The bright December sunlight streams in through the window. From library comes the roaring voice of WHITESIDE *again:* "Miss Preen! Miss Preen!"

MISS PREEN, *who is just coming through dining-room, rushes to open library doors.*

MISS PREEN. Yes, sir. Yes, sir.

WHITESIDE. (*As he, plainly in a mood, rolls himself into the room to* D.R.) Where do you disappear to all the time, My Lady Nausea?

MISS PREEN. Mr. Whiteside, I can only be in one place at a time.

WHITESIDE. That's very fortunate for this community. (MISS PREEN *goes indignantly into library and slams doors after her.* JOHN *enters from upstairs, carrying a tray of used dishes.*)

JOHN. Good morning, Mr. Whiteside. Merry Christmas.

WHITESIDE. Merry Christmas, John. Merry Christmas.

JOHN. Are you ready for your breakfast, Mr. Whiteside?

WHITESIDE. No, I don't think I want any breakfast . . . Has Miss Cutler come down yet?

JOHN. No, sir, not yet.

WHITESIDE. Is she in her room, do you know?

JOHN. Yes, sir, she is. Shall I call her?

WHITESIDE. No, no. That's all, John.

JOHN. (*Going through dining-room* U.R.) Yes, sir. (WHITESIDE, *left alone, heaves a huge sigh. Then* MAGGIE *comes down stairs. She wears a traveling suit and carries a bag.* WHITESIDE *waits for her to speak.*)

MAGGIE. (*Putting bag down* R. *of staircase.*) I'm taking the one o'clock train, Sherry. I'm leaving.

WHITESIDE. You're doing nothing of the kind!

MAGGIE. Here are your keys—your driving license. (*Hands them to him.*) The key to the safe-deposit vault is in the apartment in New York. I'll go in here now and clear things up. (*She opens library door.*)

WHITESIDE. (*Puts keys etc. in pocket.*) Just a moment, Mrs. Siddons. Where *were* you until three o'clock this morning? I sat up half the night in this station-wagon, worrying about you. You heard

64

me calling to you when you came in. Why didn't you answer me? (MAGGIE *crosses to* R. *of him.*)

MAGGIE. Look, Sherry, it's over, and you've won. I don't want to talk about it.

WHITESIDE. Oh, come, come, come, come, come. What are you trying to do—make me feel like a naughty, naughty boy? Honestly, Maggie, sometimes you can be very annoying.

MAGGIE. (*Looking at him in wonder, crossing to* L. *of him.*) You know, you're quite wonderful, Sherry, in a way. *You're* annoyed! I wish there was a laugh left in me. Shall I tell you something, Sherry? I think you are a selfish, petty egomaniac who would see his mother burned . . . at the stake . . . if that was the only way he could light his cigarette. I think you'd sacrifice your best friend without a moment's hesitation if he disturbed the sacred routine of your self-centered, paltry little life. I think you are incapable of any human emotion that goes higher up than your stomach, and I was the fool of the world for ever thinking I could trust you.

WHITESIDE. Well, as long as I live, I will never do anyone a good turn again. I won't ask you to apologize, Maggie, because in six months from now you will be thanking me instead of berating me.

MAGGIE. In six months, Sherry, I expect to be *so far away* from you— (*She is halted by a loud voice from hallway, as door bangs. "Hello—hello—hello!" It is* BERT JEFFERSON *who enters* L., *a little high.* MAGGIE *crosses* U. *to* R.)

BERT. (C.) Merry Christmas, everybody! Merry Christmas! I'm a little high, but I can explain everything. Hi, Maggie. Hi, Mr. Whiteside. Shake hands with a successful playwright. Maggie, why'd you run away last night? Where were you? Miss Sheldon thinks the play is wonderful. I read her the play and she thinks it's wonderful. Isn't that wonderful?

MAGGIE. Yes, that's fine, Bert.

BERT. Isn't that wonderful, Mr. Whiteside?

WHITESIDE. Jefferson, I think you ought to go home, don't you?

BERT. What? No—biggest day of my life. I know I'm a little drunk, but this is a big day. We've been sitting over in Billy's Tavern all night. Never realized it was daylight until it was daylight— (*Crosses to* MAGGIE R.) Listen, Maggie—Miss Sheldon says the play needs just a little bit of fixing—do it in three weeks. She's going to take me to a little place she's got in Lake Placid—just for three weeks. Going to work on the play together. Isn't it wonderful? (*A pause.*) Why don't you say something, Maggie? (*She turns away.*)

WHITESIDE. Look, Bert, I suggest you tell us all about this later. Now, why don't you—

(*He stops as* DR. BRADLEY *enters from hallway.*)

BRADLEY. (C.) Oh, excuse me! Merry Christmas, everybody. Merry Christmas.

BERT. God bless us all, and Tiny Tim.

BRADLEY. Yes . . . Mr. Whiteside, I thought perhaps if I came very early . . .

BERT. (*Crosses back of* WHITESIDE *to* BRADLEY.) You know what, Doc? I'm going to Lake Placid for three weeks—isn't that wonderful? Ever hear of Lorraine Sheldon, the famous actress? Well, we're going to Lake Placid for three weeks.

WHITESIDE. Dr. Bradley, would you do me a favor? I think Mr. Jefferson would like some black coffee and a little breakfast. Would you take care of him please?

BRADLEY. Yes, yes, of course . . .

BERT. Dr. Bradley, I'm going to buy breakfast for *you*—biggest breakfast you ever had.

BRADLEY. Yes, yes, Jefferson.

BERT. (*Putting arm about* BRADLEY, *he starts him off.*) You know what, Doctor? Let's climb down a couple of chimneys. I got a friend that doesn't believe in Santa Claus—let's climb down his chimney and frighten the hell out of him. (*He exits with* BRADLEY, L.)

WHITESIDE. Now listen to me, Maggie. I am willing to forgive your tawdry outburst and talk about this calmly.

MAGGIE. I love him so terribly. Oh, Sherry, Sherry, why did you do it? Why did you do it? (*She goes stumbling into library—closes doors after her.*)

(WHITESIDE, *left alone, looks at his watch; heaves a long sigh. Then* HARRIET *comes down steps, dressed for the street.*)

HARRIET. (*To* C.) Merry Christmas, Mr. Whiteside.

WHITESIDE. Oh! . . . Merry Christmas, Miss Stanley.

HARRIET. (*Nervously.*) I'm afraid I shouldn't be seen talking to you, Mr. Whiteside—my brother is terribly angry. I just couldn't resist asking—did you like my Christmas present?

WHITESIDE. I'm very sorry, Miss Stanley—I haven't opened it. I haven't opened any of my presents yet.

HARRIET. Oh, dear, I was so anxious to—it's right here, Mr. Whiteside. (*She goes to tree.*) Won't you open it now?

WHITESIDE. (*As he undoes string.*) I appreciate your thinking of me, Miss Stanley. This is very thoughtful of you. (*He takes out gift—an old photograph.*) Why it's lovely. I'm very fond of these old photographs. Thank you very much.

HARRIET. I was twenty-two when that was taken. That was my favorite dress . . . Do you really like it?

WHITESIDE. I do indeed. When I get back to town I shall send you a little gift.

HARRIET. Will you? Oh, thank you, Mr. Whiteside. I shall treasure it—(*She starts to go.*) Well, I shall be late for church. Good-bye. Good-bye.

WHITESIDE. Good-bye, Miss Stanley.

(*As she goes out front door* WHITESIDE'S *eyes return to gift. He puzzles over it for a second, shakes his head. Mumbles to himself—* "*What is there about that woman?" Shakes his head again in perplexity.*) (JOHN *comes from dining-room, carrying a breakfast tray.*)

JOHN. Sarah's got a little surprise for you, Mr. Whiteside. She's just taking it out of the oven. (*Crossing from* U.R. *to upstairs.*)

WHITESIDE. Thank you, John. (JOHN *disappears up stairs.*) (*Then suddenly there is a great ringing of the doorbell. It stops for a second, then picks up violently again.*) Miss Preen! Miss Preen! (MISS PREEN *comes hurrying from library.*)

MISS PREEN. Yes, sir. Yes, sir.

WHITESIDE. Answer the door, will you? John is upstairs. (MISS PREEN, *obviously annoyed, hurries to door.*) (WHITESIDE *puts package in chair basket.*) (*We hear her voice from hallway "Who is it?" An answering male voice:* "*Polly Adler's!" Then a little shriek from* MISS PREEN, *and in a moment we see the reason why. She is carried into the room in the arms of a pixie-like gentleman, who is kissing her over and over.*)

THE GENTLEMAN. (*Carrying* MISS PREEN.) (*Coming* D.C.) I love you madly—madly. Did you hear what I said—madly! Kiss me. Again! Don't be afraid of my passion. Kiss me! I can feel the hot blood pounding through your varicose veins.

MISS PREEN. (*Through all this.*) Put me down! Put me down! Do you hear? Don't you dare kiss me! Who are you! Put me down or I'll scream. Mr. Whiteside! Mr. Whiteside!

WHITESIDE. Banjo, for God's sake! Banjo!

BANJO. Hello, Whiteside. Will you sign for this package, please?

MISS PREEN. Mr. Whiteside!

WHITESIDE. Banjo, put that woman down. That is my nurse, you mental delinquent.

67

BANJO. (*Putting* MISS PREEN *on her feet.*) Come to my room in half an hour and bring some rye bread. (*Slaps* MISS PREEN'S *fanny.*)

MISS PREEN. (*Outraged.*) Really, Mr. Whiteside! (*She adjusts her clothes with a quick jerk or two and marches into library—closes doors.*) (JOHN, *at the same time, comes hurrying down stairs;* BANJO *beckons to him. Bending his leg and raising it,* BANJO *puts it in* JOHN'S *hand. Amazed,* JOHN *rushes off* U.R.)

BANJO. (*Crosses to* C.) Whiteside, I'm here to spend Christmas with you. Give me a kiss.

WHITESIDE. Get away from me, you reform school fugitive. How did you get here anyway?

BANJO. (C.) Darryl Zanuck loaned me his reindeer. Whiteside, we finished shooting the picture yesterday and I'm on my way to Nova Scotia. Flew here in twelve hours—borrowed an airplane from Howard Hughes. Whiteside, I brought you a wonderful Christmas present. (*He produces a little tissue-wrapped package. Crosses to* WHITESIDE.) This brassiere was once worn by Hedy Lamarr. (*Dropping it in* WHITESIDE'S *lap.*)

WHITESIDE. Listen, you idiot, how long can you stay?

BANJO. Just long enough to take a bath. I'm on my way to Nova Scotia. Where's Maggie?

WHITESIDE. Nova Scotia? What are you going to Nova Scotia for?

BANJO. I'm sick of Hollywood and there's a dame in New York I don't want to see. So I figured I'd go to Nova Scotia and get some smoked salmon . . . Where the hell's Maggie? I want to see her . . . What's the matter with you? Where is she?

WHITESIDE. Banjo, I'm glad you're here. I'm very annoyed at Maggie. Very!

BANJO. What's the matter?

(WHITESIDE *rises, crosses to* L.) Say, what is this? I thought you couldn't walk. (*Crossing to* C.)

WHITESIDE. Oh, I've been all right for weeks. That isn't the point. I'm furious at Maggie. She's turned on me like a viper. You know how fond I am of her. Well, after these years she's repaying my affection by behaving like a fishwife.

BANJO. What are you talking about?

WHITESIDE. (*A step* L.) But I never believed for a moment she was really in love with him.

BANJO. In love with who? I just got here—remember? (BUSINESS *of pointing to himself.*)

WHITESIDE. (*Pace* L.) Great God, I'm telling you, you Hollywood nitwit. A young newspaper man here in town.

BANJO. Maggie finally fell—well, what do you know? What kind of a guy is he?

WHITESIDE. (*Crosses to him.*) Oh, shut up and listen, will you?

BANJO. Well, go on. What happened?

WHITESIDE. (*Pacing* L.) Well, Lorraine Sheldon happened to come out here and visit me.

BANJO. Old hot-pants—here?

WHITESIDE. (*Back to* BANJO.) Now listen! This young fellow, he'd written a play. You can guess the rest. He's going away with Lorraine this afternoon. To "rewrite." So there you are. Maggie's in there now, crying her eyes out. (*Crosses to sofa—sits.*)

BANJO. (*Crosses* L.) Gee! . . . Say, wait a minute. What do you mean Lorraine Sheldon happened to come out here? I smell a rat, Sherry—a rat with a beard.

WHITESIDE. Well, all right, all right. But I did it for Maggie—because I thought it was the right thing for *her*.

BANJO. (*Crosses* R.) Oh, sure. You haven't thought of yourself in years . . . Gee, poor kid. Can I go in and talk to her?

WHITESIDE. No—no. Leave her alone.

BANJO. (*Crosses* L.) Any way I could help, Sherry? Where's this guy live—this guy she likes? Can we get hold of him?

WHITESIDE. (*Rises—crosses to* BANJO.) Now wait a minute, Banjo. We don't want any phony warrants, or you pretending to be J. Edgar Hoover. I've been through all that with you before. (*He paces again* L.) I got Lorraine out here and I've got to get her away.

BANJO. It's got to be good, Sherry. Lorraine's no dope. (*Crosses* U.R.) . . . Now, there must be *some*thing that would get her out of here like a bat out of hell. (*Crosses to* L.) Say! I think I've got it! That fellow she's so crazy about over in England—what's his name again?—Lord Fanny or whatever it is. Bottomley—that's it! Bottomley!

WHITESIDE. (*With a pained expression.*) No, Banjo. No.

BANJO. Wait a minute—you don't catch on. We send Lorraine a cablegram from Lord Bottomley—

WHITESIDE. I catch on, Banjo. Lorraine caught on too. It's been tried.

BANJO. (*Crosses* R.) Oh! . . . I told you she was no dope . . . (*He sits in wheelchair.*) Well, we've got a tough proposition on your hands.

WHITESIDE. The trouble is there's so damned little time. Get out of my chair! (WHITESIDE *sits in chair as* BANJO *gets out of it and crosses to* C.) Lorraine's taking him away with her this afternoon. Oh, damn, damn, damn. There must be some way out. The trouble is I've done this job too well. Hell and damnation!

BANJO. (C.) Stuck, huh?

WHITESIDE. In the words of one of our greatest lyric poets, you said it.

BANJO. Yeh. Gee, I'm hungry. We'll think of something, Sherry— you watch. We'll get Lorraine out of here if I have to do it one piece at a time. (SARAH *enters from dining-room, bearing a tray on which reposes the culinary surprise which* JOHN *has mentioned which she is hiding behind her back.*)

SARAH. (*To* L. *of chair.*) Merry Christmas, Mr. Whiteside . . . Excuse me. (*This last is to* BANJO.) I've got something for you . . . (BANJO *lifts the latest delicacy and proceeds to eat it as she presents the empty plate to* WHITESIDE.)

SARAH. But, Mr. Whiteside, it was for you.

WHITESIDE. Never mind, Sarah. He's quite mad.

BANJO. Come, Petrushka, we shall dance. We shall dance in the snow! (*He clutches* SARAH *and waltzes her toward kitchen* U.R., *loudly humming the Merry Widow Waltz.*)

SARAH. (*As she is borne away.*) Mr. Whiteside! Mr. Whiteside!

WHITESIDE. Just give him some breakfast, Sarah. He's harmless. (WHITESIDE *barely has a moment in which to collect his thoughts before library doors are opened and* MISS PREEN *emerges. She is dressed for the street and carries a bag.*) (*She plants herself to* L. *of* WHITESIDE, *puts down her bag and starts drawing on a pair of gloves.*)

And just what does this mean?

MISS PREEN. (C.) It means, Mr. Whiteside, that I am leaving. My address is on the desk inside, you can send me a check.

WHITESIDE. You realize, Miss Preen, that this is completely unprofessional?

MISS PREEN. I do indeed. I am not only walking out on this case, Mr. Whiteside, but I am leaving the nursing profession. I became a nurse because all my life, ever since I was a little girl, I was filled with the idea of serving a suffering humanity. After one month with you, Mr. Whiteside, I am going to work in a munitions factory. From now on anything that I can do to help exterminate the human race will fill me with the greatest of pleasure. If Florence Nightingale had ever nursed you, Mr. Whiteside, she would have married

70

Jack the Ripper instead of founding the Red Cross. Good day. (*She goes* U.L.) (MRS. STANLEY, *in a state of great fluttery excitement, rushes down the stairs.*)

MRS. STANLEY. (*Headed for front door* L.) Mr. Stanley is here with June. He's brought June back. Thank goodness, *thank goodness.* (*We hear her at door.*) June, June, thank God you're back! You're not married, are you?

JUNE. (*From hallway.*) No, Mother, I'm not. And please don't be hysterical. (*Then* MRS. STANLEY *comes into view, her arms around a rebellious* JUNE. *Behind them looms* STANLEY, *every inch the stern father.*)

MRS. STANLEY. (L.) Oh, June, if it had been anyone but that awful boy. Thank goodness you stopped it, Ernest; how did you do it?

STANLEY. (D.L.) Never mind that, Daisy. Just take June upstairs. I have something to say to Mr. Whiteside.

MRS. STANLEY. What about Richard? Is there any news?

STANLEY. It's all right, Daisy—all under control. Just take June upstairs.

JUNE. Father, haven't we had enough melodrama? I don't have to be taken upstairs—I'll go upstairs . . . Merry Christmas, Mr. Whiteside. It looks bad for John L. Lewis. Come on, Mother—lock me in my room.

MRS. STANLEY. Now, June, you'll feel much better after you've had a hot bath, I know. Have you had anything to eat? (*She follows her daughter up stairs.* STANLEY *turns to* WHITESIDE.)

STANLEY. (*Crosses to* C.) I am pleased to inform you, sir, that your plans for my daughter seem to have gone a trifle awry. She is not, nor will she ever be, married to that Labor agitator that you so kindly picked out for her. As for my son, he has been apprehended in Toledo, and will be brought home within the hour. Not having your gift for invective, sir, I cannot tell you what I think of your obnoxious interference in my affairs, but I have now arranged that you will interfere no longer (*He turns toward hallway.*) Come in, gentlemen. (*Two burly* MEN *come into view and stand in archway* L.) Mr. Whiteside, these gentlemen are deputy sheriffs. They have a warrant by which I am enabled to put you out of this house, and I need hardly add that it will be the greatest moment of my life. Mr. Whiteside—(*He looks at his watch.*) I am giving you fifteen minutes in which to pack up and get out. If you are not gone in fifteen minutes, Mr. Whiteside, these gentlemen will forcibly eject you. (*He turns to* DEPUTIES.) Thank you, gentlemen. Will

71

you wait outside, please? (*The* MEN *file out.*) Fifteen minutes, Mr. Whiteside—and that means bag, baggage, wheelchair, penguins, octopus and cockroaches. (*Crossing up to stairs.*) I am now going upstairs to smash our radio, so that not even accidentally will I ever hear your voice again.

WHITESIDE. Sure you don't want my autograph, old fellow?

STANLEY. Fifteen minutes, Mr. Whiteside. (*And he goes upstairs.*)

BANJO. (*Enter* U.R., *hanging hat on tree branch, he crosses to* C.) Say, can she cook. Well, Whiteside, I didn't get an idea. Any news from the front?

WHITESIDE. Yes. The enemy is at my rear, and nibbling.

BANJO. (*Crossing toward* WHITESIDE.) Where'd you say Maggie was? In there?

WHITESIDE. It's no use, Banjo. She's taking the one o'clock train out.

BANJO. No kidding? You didn't tell me that. You mean she's quitting you, after all these years? She's really leaving?

WHITESIDE. She is!

BANJO. That means you've only got till one o'clock to do something?

WHITESIDE. No, dear. I have exactly fifteen minutes—(*He looks at his watch.*) ah—fourteen minutes—in which to pull out of my hat the God-damnedest rabbit you have ever seen.

BANJO. What do you mean fifteen minutes?

WHITESIDE. In exactly fifteen minutes Baby's rosy little body is being tossed into the snow. Mine host has sworn out a warrant. I am being kicked out.

BANJO. What? I never heard of such a thing. What would he do a thing like that for?

WHITESIDE. Never mind, never mind. The point is, I have only fifteen minutes. Banjo dear, the master is growing a little desperate.

BANJO. (*Paces a moment.*) What about laying your cards on the table with Lorraine?

WHITESIDE. Now, Banjo. You know Dream Girl as well as I do. What do *you* think?

BANJO. You're right.

WHITESIDE. (*Wearily.*) Banjo, go in and talk to Maggie for a minute—right in there. I want to think.

BANJO. (*Crossing* R.) Say! If I knew where Lorraine *was*, I could get a car and run her over. It wouldn't hurt her much.

WHITESIDE. Please, Banjo. I've got to think.

72

BANJO. (*Opening library doors.*) Pardon me, Miss, is this the Y.M.C.A.? (*The doors close.* WHITESIDE *is alone again. He leans back, concentrating intensely. He shakes his head as, one after another, he discards a couple of ideas.*) (*We hear outer door open and close, and from hallway comes* RICHARD. *Immediately behind him is a stalwart looking* MAN *with an air of authority. They cross to below staircase.*)

MAN. (*To* RICHARD, *as he indicates* WHITESIDE.) Is this your father?

RICHARD. (C.) No, you idiot . . . Hello, Mr. Whiteside. I didn't get very far. Any suggestions?

WHITESIDE. I'm very sorry, Richard—very sorry indeed. I wish I were in a position—

STANLEY. (*Descending stairs.*) Well, you're *not* in position . . . Thank you very much, officer. Here's a little something for your trouble.

MAN. Thank you, sir. Good-day. (*He goes out* L.)

STANLEY. Will you go upstairs, please, Richard? (RICHARD *hesitates a second. Looks at his father, then at* WHITESIDE; *silently goes up steps.*) (STANLEY *follows him, but pauses on landing.*) Ten minutes, Mr. Whiteside. (*And he goes.*) (*Immediately* JOHN *enters from dining-room, bringing a glass of orange-juice on a tray.*)

JOHN. (*Down to* L. *of* WHITESIDE.) I brought you some orange-juice Mr. Whiteside. Feeling any better?

WHITESIDE. Superb, John. Any cyanide in this orange-juice? (*The door-bell rings.*) Open the door, John.

JOHN. Yes, sir.

WHITESIDE. It's probably some mustard gas from an old friend.

JOHN. (*En route to door* L.) Say, that crazy fellow made a great hit with Sarah. He wants to give her a *screen test.* (*At outer door we hear* LORRAINE'S *voice:* "Good morning—Is Mr. Whiteside up yet?" JOHN'S *answer:* "Yes, he is, Miss Sheldon—he's right here.")

WHITESIDE. Uhh—

LORRAINE. (*Entering, in a very smart Christmas morning costume.*) Merry Christmas, darling! Merry Christmas! I've come to have Christmas breakfast with you, my dear. May I? (*She kisses him.* JOHN *coming to* R. *of chair, takes empty glass from* WHITESIDE.)

WHITESIDE. (*Nothing matters any more.*) Of course, my Sprite. John, a tray for Miss Sheldon—better make it one-minute eggs. (*John en route to dining-room and exit.*)

LORRAINE. (*Crossing to* C.) Sherry, it's the most perfect Christmas

73

morning—the snow is absolutely glistening. Too bad you can't get out.

WHITESIDE. Oh, I'll probably see a bit of it . . . I hear you're off for Lake Placid, my Blossom. What time are you going?

LORRAINE. Oh, Sherry, how did you know? Is Bert here?

WHITESIDE. No, he rolled in a little while ago. Worked rather fast, didn't you, dear?

LORRAINE. (*A step to* L.) Darling, I was just swept off my feet by the play—it's fantastically good. Sherry, it's the kind of part that only comes along once in ten years. I'm so grateful to you, darling. Really, Sherry, sometimes I think that you're the only friend I have in the world. (*Crossing to* WHITESIDE.)

WHITESIDE. Thank you, dear. What time did you say you were leaving—you and Jefferson?

LORRAINE. (*Crosses to sofa.*) Oh, I don't know—I think it's four o'clock You know, quite apart from anything else, Sherry, Bert is really a very attractive man. It makes it rather a pleasure squaring accounts with little Miss Vitriol. (*Sits on sofa.*) In fact, it's all worked out beautifully . . . Sherry lamb, I want to give you the most beautiful Christmas present you've ever had in your life. Now what do you want? Anything! I'm so deliriously happy that—(*A laugh comes from library. She stops.*) That sounds like Banjo. Is he here?

WHITESIDE. He is, my dear. Just the family circle gathering at Christmas. (*A look at his watch.*) My, how time flies when you're having fun. (BANJO *emerges from library, closes doors.*)

BANJO. (*Crosses to* C.) Why, hello, Sweetie Pants. How are you?

LORRAINE. (*Not over-cordial.*) Very well, thank you. And you, Banjo?

BANJO. I'm fine, fine. How's the mattress business, Lorraine?

LORRAINE. *Very* funny. It's too bad, Banjo, that your pictures aren't as funny as you seem to think *you* are.

BANJO. (C.) You've got me there, Mama. Say, you look in the pink, Lorraine . . . Anything in the wind, Whiteside?

WHITESIDE. Not a glimmer.

BANJO. What time does the boat sail?

WHITESIDE. Ten minutes.

LORRAINE. What boat is this?

BANJO. The good ship Up the Creek. (MAGGIE *emerges from library, a sheaf of papers in her hand. She stops.*)

MAGGIE. I've listed everything except the New Year's Eve broad-

74

cast. Wasn't there a schedule on that?

WHITESIDE. (*Uneasily.*) I think it's on the table there, some place.

MAGGIE. Thank you. (*She turns to papers on table.*)

LORRAINE. (*Obviously for MAGGIE'S ears.*) New Year's Eve? Oh, Bert and I'll hear it in Lake Placid. You were at my cottage up there once, weren't you, Sherry? It's lovely, isn't it? Away from everything. Just snow and clear, cold night.

(*The door-bell rings.*)

LORRAINE. Oh, that's probably Bert now. I told him to meet me here. (MAGGIE, *as though she had not heard a word, goes quietly into library, closing doors after her.* JOHN *enters swing-door* U.L.) You know, I'm looking forward to Lake Placid. Bert's the kind of man who will do all winter sports beautifully.

BANJO. (*Crosses* D.L.) Will he get time? (LORRAINE *rises, crosses to* U.R.) (*Loud voices are heard from hallway, and* JOHN *backs into the room, obviously directing a major operation.*)

EXPRESSMAN. Whiteside?

JOHN. Yes, sir.

EXPRESSMAN. American Express!

JOHN. All right—come ahead. Care now—careful—right in here.

LORRAINE. Why, Sherry, what's this? (*Into view come two* EXPRESSMEN, *groaning and grunting under the weight of nothing more or less than a huge mummy-case.*)

EXPRESSMAN. Careful there. Now swing your end. Where do you want this put? (LORRAINE *crosses to* R. *of wheelchair.*)

JOHN. Right there. (EXPRESSMEN *put mummy-case* U.C. *below* R. *newel post.*) It's for you, Mr. Whiteside.

WHITESIDE. Dear God, if there was one thing I needed right now it was an Egyptian mummy. (EXPRESSMEN *go* L. JOHN *exits up* L.)

BANJO. (*Crossing to mummy, reads tag on case.*) "Merry Christmas from the Khedive of Egypt." What did you send *him?* Grant's tomb? (STANLEY *has descended the stairs in time to witness this newest hue and cry.*)

STANLEY. Five minutes, Mr. Whiteside. (*He indicates mummy-case.*) Including that. (*And up the stairs again.*)

LORRAINE. Why, what was all that about? Who is that man?

WHITESIDE. He announces the time every few minutes. (BANJO *sits on sofa.*) I pay him a small sum.

LORRAINE. But what on earth *for,* Sherry?

WHITESIDE. (*Violently.*) I lost my watch. (*From hallway a familiar figure peeps in.*)

75

BRADLEY. (*Crossing* R.) Oh, excuse me, Mr. Whiteside, I see you're busy.

WHITESIDE. (*Closing his eyes.*) Good God!

BRADLEY. (*Coming into room—tips his hat to mummy, realizes his mistake.*) Pardon me, I'll wait in here. I've written a new chapter on the left kidney. (*He smiles apologetically at* LORRAINE *and* BANJO, *goes into library* D.R.)

LORRAINE. Is that the plumber again, Sherry? (*Crosses to* L.C.) Oh, dear, I wonder where Bert is . . . Darling, you're not very Christmasy—you're usually bubbling over on Christmas morning. Who sent this to you, Sherry—the Khedive of Egypt? You know, I think it's rather beautiful. I must go to Egypt some day—I really must. I know I'd love it. The first time I went to Pompeii I cried all night. All those people—all those lives. Where are they now? (*BANJO doesn't know. He shrugs his shoulders.*) Sherry! Don't you ever think about that? I do. Here was a woman—like myself—a woman who once lived and loved, full of the same passions, fears, jealousies, hates. And what remains of any of it now? Just this, and nothing more. (*She opens case, then, with a sudden impulse, steps into it and folds her arms, mummy-fashion.*) A span of four thousand years—a mere atom in the eternity of time—and here am I, another woman living out her life. I want to cry. (*She closes her eyes, and as she stands there, immobilized, the eyes of* BANJO *and* WHITESIDE *meet. The same idea has leaped into their minds.* BANJO, *rising slowly from couch, starts to approach mummy-case, casually whistling "Dixie." But just before he reaches it* LORRAINE *steps blandly out.* BANJO *circles below couch to back of it.*) Oh, I mustn't talk this way today. It's Christmas! It's Christmas! (*BANJO back of sofa.*)

WHITESIDE. (*Pure charm.*) Lorraine dear, have you ever played St. Joan?

LORRAINE. No, I haven't, Sherry. What makes you ask that?

WHITESIDE. There was something about your expression as you stood in that case—there was an absolute halo about you.

LORRAINE. Why, Sherry, how sweet!

WHITESIDE. (*BANJO eases* R.) It transcended any mortal expression I've ever seen. Step into it again, dear.

LORRAINE. Sherry, you're joshing me—aren't you?

WHITESIDE. My dear, I don't make light of these things. I was deeply moved. There was a strange beauty about you, Lorraine—pure da Vinci. Please do it again.

LORRAINE. (*As she approaches case,* BANJO *takes three steps toward it.*) Well, I don't know exactly what it was that I did, but I'll—(*She starts to step into case again, then turns.*) Oh, I feel too silly, Sherry. (*Crosses down to* WHITESIDE.)

WHITESIDE. Lorraine, dear, in that single moment you approached the epitome of your art, and you should not be ashamed of it. You asked me a little while ago what I wanted for a Christmas present. All that I want, Lorraine, is the memory of you in that mummy-case.

LORRAINE. Why, darling, I'm—all choked up. (*Crossing her arms, she takes a moment to throw herself in the mood, circles slowly* U.C., *then steps reverently into the case.*) "Dust thou art, and dust to dust—" Banjo! (*Bang!* BANJO *has closed case and fastened it.* WHITESIDE *leaps out of the chair.*)

WHITESIDE. Eureka!

BANJO. (*They shake hands.*) There's service for you!

WHITESIDE. Will she be all right in there?

BANJO. Sure—she can breathe easy. I'll let her out as soon as we get on the plane . . . What are we going to do now? Say, how do we get this out of here?

WHITESIDE. One thing at a time—that's the next step.

BANJO. Think fast, Captain. Think fast. (*And* MAGGIE *enters from library, papers in hand.* WHITESIDE *leaps back to his chair,* BANJO *sits on arm of couch.*)

MAGGIE. (L.C.) This is everything, Sherry—I'm leaving three carbons. Is there anything out there? What's in this basket?

WHITESIDE. (*Eager to be rid of her.*) Nothing at all. Thank you, thank you.

MAGGIE. (*Delving into basket.*) Shall I file these letters? Do you want this picture?

WHITESIDE. No—throw everything away. Wait—give me the picture. I want the picture.

MAGGIE. (*Handing him picture.*) The only thing I haven't done is to put all your broadcasts in order. Do you want me to do that?

WHITESIDE. (*A flash of recollection has come to him as he takes* HARRIET'S *photograph in his hand, but he contrives to smother his excitement.*) What? . . . Ah—do that, will you? Do it right away—it's very important. Right away, Maggie.

MAGGIE. I'll see you before I go, Banjo. (*She goes into library again, closing doors.*)

WHITESIDE. (*Watching her out, then rising.*) I've got it.

BANJO. (*Rising.*) What?

77

WHITESIDE. I knew I'd seen this face before. Now I know how to get this out of here.

BANJO. What face? How? (*And at that instant,* STANLEY *comes down stairs, watch in hand.*)

STANLEY. (*Coming* D.C.) The time is up, Mr. Whiteside. Fifteen minutes. (BANJO *crosses* R.)

WHITESIDE. (*Crosses to* C.) Ah, yes, Mr. Stanley. Fifteen minutes. But just one favor before I go. I would like you to summon those two officers and ask them to help this gentleman down to the airport with this mummy-case. Would you be good enough to do that, Mr. Stanley?

STANLEY. I will do nothing of the kind.

WHITESIDE. Oh, I think you will, Mr. Stanley. Or I shall inform my radio audience, on my next broadcast, that your sister, Harriet Stanley, is none other than the famous Harriet Sedley, who murdered her mother and father with an axe twenty-five years ago in Gloucester, Massachusetts . . . (STANLEY *sinks into sofa.*) Come, Mr. Stanley, it's a very small favor. Or would you rather have the good folk of Mesalia repeating at your very doorstep that once popular little jingle:
"Harriet Sedley took an axe
And gave her mother forty whacks,
And when the job was nicely done,
She gave her father forty-one."
Remember, Mr. Stanley, I too am giving up something. It would make a hell of a broadcast . . . Well?

STANLEY. (*Rises, crosses to piano* D.L.) Mr. Whiteside, you are the damnedest person I have ever met.

WHITESIDE. You're a little late in finding that out. Officers, will you come in here, please?

BANJO. (*To case.*) Whiteside, you're a *great* man. (*And he kisses his hand and pats case.*) (*Takes hat from Christmas tree.*)

WHITESIDE. (*As* DEPUTIES *enter* L.) Come right in, officers. Mr. Stanley would like you to help this gentleman down to the airport with this mummy-case . . . He is sending it to a friend in Nova Scotia.

BANJO. Collect. (DEPUTIES *cross to case and pick it up.*)

WHITESIDE. Right, Mr. Stanley?

STANLEY. Yes . . . Yes.

WHITESIDE. Thank you, gentlemen—handle it carefully . . . Banjo, my love, you're wonderful and I may write a book about you.

BANJO. Don't bother—I can't read. (*To* MAGGIE, *as she enters from library.*) Good-bye, Maggie—love conquers all . . . Don't drop that case, boys—it contains an *antique*. (*And he goes, following* DEPUTIES *and mummy-case off* L.)

MAGGIE. (*To* C.) Sherry! Sherry, was that—?

WHITESIDE. It was indeed. (*Sees fur muff* LORRAINE *has left on couch back. Presents it to* MAGGIE.) Oh—a little Christmas present for you.

MAGGIE. Sherry! Sherry, you old reprobate!

WHITESIDE. Just send me a necktie some time. My hat and coat, Maggie, I am leaving for New York.

MAGGIE. You're leaving, Sherry?

WHITESIDE. Don't argue, Rat Girl—do as you're told.

MAGGIE. Yes, Mr. Whiteside. (*She goes into library as* BERT *comes running in from hallway, breathless.*)

BERT. (*To* C.) Mr. Whiteside, I want to apologize—(*His eyes encounter the very healthy* WHITESIDE.) Say!

WHITESIDE. Don't give it a thought, Bert. There's been a slight change of plan. Miss Sheldon is off on a world cruise—I am taking your play to Katherine Cornell.

(MAGGIE *enters from library with* WHITESIDE'S *coat and hat and cane.*)

Miss Cutler will explain everything.

BERT. Maggie!

WHITESIDE. Thank you, Maggie, my darling. (*As she assists* WHITESIDE *with his coat.*) (*The* DOCTOR *comes hurrying out of library.*)

BRADLEY. (*To below wheelchair.*) Mr. Whiteside, are you very busy?

WHITESIDE. Ah, yes, Doctor, yes. Very busy. But if you ever get to New York, Doctor, try and find me . . . Good-bye, my lamb. I love you very much.

MAGGIE. Sherry, you're wonderful.

WHITESIDE. (*Shakes hands.*) Nonsense . . . Good-bye, Jefferson. You'll never know the trouble you've caused.

BERT. Good-bye, Mr. Whiteside. (*Crosses to* MAGGIE.)

WHITESIDE. (*Crosses* L.) Good-bye, Mr. Stanley. I would like to hear, in the near future, that your daughter has married her young man and that your son has been permitted to follow his own bent. OR ELSE . . . Merry Christmas, *everybody!* (*He exits* L.)

BERT. Maggie, for God's sake, what *is* all this? Where's he going? I didn't know he could walk even.

MAGGIE. It's all right. Bert. You're too young to know. Just don't ask questions.

MRS. STANLEY. (*Descending stairs.*) Ernest, Richard's being very difficult. You'll have to talk to him. (*There is a loud crash on porch, followed by an anguished yell.*)

WHITESIDE. Owww—God damn it!

MAGGIE. Bert! Doctor!

BERT. (*As he and* DOCTOR *run off* L.) Something's happened!

(*Enter down the stairs* RICHARD *and* JUNE.)

RICHARD. What's the matter? What's wrong?

JUNE. Has something happened? What is it?

MRS. STANLEY. Oh, dear! Oh, dear!

WHITESIDE. (*Off stage.*) Miss Preen! . . . (*Into view come* BERT *and* BRADLEY, *carrying* WHITESIDE.) Miss Preen! I want Miss Preen back! (*As* WHITESIDE *is carried past* L. *newel post, the Curtain Starts Down.*)

MAGGIE. Sherry, Sherry, oh my poor Sherry!

MRS. STANLEY. (*She faints.*) Ohhhh!

SARAH. (*Entering from* U.R. *with* JOHN.) What's the matter? What is it? Oh, dear!

DR. BRADLEY. Bring that chair right over! Bring that chair!

JUNE. Mother! Mother!

BERT. That's all right, Mr. Whiteside. Just relax!

MR. STANLEY. Oh! Oh!

RICHARD. What's the matter, Mother?

(STANLEY *is beating his hands on piano and tearing his hair.* MRS. STANLEY *has fainted on stairway.* WHITESIDE *is about to be put in wheelchair again by* BERT *and* DOCTOR BRADLEY *as*

THE CURTAIN IS DOWN

(Medium)

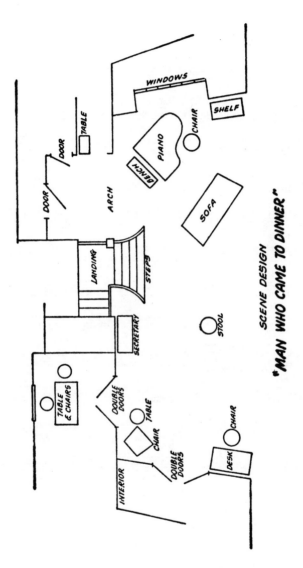

SCENE DESIGN

"MAN WHO CAME TO DINNER"

What Am I To Do

C. Porter.

PROPERTY PLOT

Act I, Scene 1

Desk chest, D.R. with: telephone, candy box, vase with flowers, ash-tray, cigarette box

Bowl of gardenias

High-boy, U.C., with: two silver candlesticks, vase with lilies of the valley, two pictures, books, bust.

Round table, R. of stair rail, with: one lamp, candy jar, gew-gaw, cigarette box

Table, against stairway in alcove, U., with: silver platter, two silver candlesticks

Grandfather clock, U.R., corner of alcove

Three-cornered table, U.L. corner of alcove, with: two gew-gaws, vase with laurel

Round table, U.L., with: two pictures, ash-tray, two cigarette boxes, lamp

Piano, D.L., with: picture, ash-tray, Chinese vase, six song sheets, cigarette box, vase with wheat and Japanese lanterns

Magazine rack D.L. against wall, with: two ash-trays, two gew-gaws, magazines (six)

Table, in back of sofa, with: book, ash-tray, cigarette box

Pair of gold brackets with ivy in vases on either side of window, L.

HAND PROPS

Steno-pad (MAGGIE), small

Pencil (MAGGIE)

One opened letter (MAGGIE)

Set of six opened letters typed with message from Whiteside, dialogue (cables) (MAGGIE)

Box of pills (PREEN)

Tray with: glass of water, cup and saucer (PREEN)

Doctor's bag with: thick manuscript (BRADLEY)

Dinner menu in basket of wheelchair (WHITESIDE)

Pen, letter (MAGGIE)

2 dinner glasses (JOHN)

Cornflakes in bowl, spoon on tray (PREEN)

Orange juice in pitcher with glass on tray (SARAH)

2 pillows with white cases (JOHN)

2 large brown wrapped packages

3 cablegrams, 1 telegram (with message "Treacle face") (RICHARD)

Plant (wrapped) (MRS. DEXTER)

Jelly jar (wrapped) (MRS. MCCUTCHEON)

Time Magazine (MRS. MCCUTCHEON)

Cigarettes (RICHARD)

Large spray holly (HARRIET)

Roach City (METZ)

2 pair handcuffs (CONVICTS)

1 rifle (BAKER)

Wheel-chair off R.

Wrist watch for WHITESIDE

Act I, Scene 2

Small side table to L. of chair U.R. corner with: red rose in silver bowl

4 cablegrams in basket of wheelchair

Roach City R. of wheel-chair with: telephone, empty candy box, book

Crumpled manuscript paper on floor L. of wheel-chair

Cardboard box with: 2 books on floor L. of wheel-chair

3 books open face down on floor L. of wheel-chair

2 stacks of books on desk chest D.R.

Manuscript paper and letters, on desk chest D.R.

1 book face down on sofa L.

3 stacks of books on table back of sofa

Lilies of the valley (struck) and pinks put in

HAND PROPS

Bottle of medicine (PREEN)
2 glasses with dark liquid (PREEN)
Towel (PREEN)
Tray with: little cakes (SARAH)

Prop table off stairs
Album photographs (HARRIET)
Telephone bill (MR. STANLEY)

Prop table off L.
2 pair ice skates (shoes) (RICHARD and JUNE)
Candid camera with strap (RICHARD)
Play script in envelope (MAGGIE)

ACT II

2 stacks of books on desk chest D.R.

Correspondence on D.R. desk chest

Radio script on D.R. desk chest
Christmas tree center with: about 30 Christmas wrapped packages under tree

Fountain pen on desk chest D.R.

Time table D.R. chest desk
Book on table back of sofa D.L.
Ottoman (large one) with: ashtray, pencil, 2 air mail letters (unopened)
Cigarette box on piano, open
Fir wreath on window L.
Holly in vase on hall table R.
Mistletoe over dining-room door

IN DINING ROOM

Holly wreath on window
Silver bowl with doily (same as

Act I, Scene 2)

HAND PROPS

2 Christmas packages (JOHN)
2 Christmas packages (SARAH)
Wheel-chair with: copy of Broadcast (radio script) in basket
Pillow cases, sheets (JOHN)
Basin, benzoin inhalator, hot water bag (PREEN)
Tray with 4 cocktails (JEFFERSON)
Christmas package with old photographs (HARRIET)
Small suitcase (JUNE)

Man's small suitcase, 2 cameras with straps (RICHARD)
3 Christmas packages (MRS. STANLEY)
Letter opened (MR. STANLEY)
Letter opened (MRS. STANLEY)
Small crate with 4 penguins with tag
6 photographs (4 x 6) (RICHARD)
2 standing microphones
Portable radio control board,

87

mouthpiece, earphones (electric)
Out of town newspapers
(folded) (JEFFERSON)
2 broadcast copies (radio scripts) (WESTCOTT)
Letter in envelope unsealed
(BEVERLY)

HAND PROPS

ACT III

Sheaf of papers (MAGGIE)
Cake on plate (SARAH)
Glass of orange juice on tray
(JOHN)
Breakfast tray (JOHN)
Kitchen cooking apron (SARAH)

Woman's suitcase, keys on key
ring, driver's license (MAGGIE)
Small Christmas package
(BANJO)
MUMMY

SUGGESTED TEXT CHANGES

With the consent of the authors, we suggest below a few minor changes in the text of this play. By making these changes, high schools and similar groups will find it considerably easier to produce it before audiences which may consider the original version a bit too "advanced" or "sophisticated."

(There is a little smoking here and there which can easily be omitted.)

Page 11. 2nd line from top of page omit "sex-starved," substitute "slimy." 5th line from bottom of page omit "to have a baby!"

P. 12. 14th line from bottom of page omit "Navel," substitute "belt."

P. 13. 14th line from bottom of page omit "brassieres" and substitute "girdles."

P. 14. 17th line from bottom of page omit "fawn's behind," substitute "horse's neck."

P. 15. 14th line from bottom of page omit "sex." 4th line from bottom of page, omit "bordello."

P. 16. 17th line from top of page add "bootlegging." 18th line omit "white slavery."

P. 19. 15th line from bottom of page omit "in one of the booths," substitute "big as life."

P. 20. 5th line from bottom of page omit "What can go wrong? They're in there." 4th line from bottom of page, omit entirely. Last line on page omit "maternity."

P. 24. 16th line from top of page omit "A sailor?" 22nd line from top of page omit "sex," substitute "handwashing." 21st line from top of page omit "life."

P. 26. 7th line from top of page omit entirely.

P. 27. 2nd line from bottom of page omit "sex-ridden" and "Alley," substitute for latter, "Mooning." Last line on page omit "catting."

P. 28. 12th line from top of page omit "haylofts," substitute "hidden by-ways." 22nd line from top of page omit "This is merely delayed puberty."

P. 29. 16th line from top of page omit "I'll get the ants out of those." 17th line from top of page omit entirely.

P. 32. 16th line from top of page omit "God," substitute "I declare."

P. 33. 19th line from top of page omit "God damnedest," substitute "goldarnedest."

P. 39. 13th line from bottom of page omit "God damn it," substitute "Confound it."

P. 41. 2nd line from top of page omit "Who's in," substitute "How's."

P. 42. 2nd line from bottom of page omit "fanny," substitute "anatomy."

P. 43. 19th and 20th lines from top of page omit "and you could absolutely see Trafalgar Square." 14th, 13th, 12th and 11th lines from bottom of page omit everything beginning "I don't," down to but not including "What about." 8th and 7th lines from bottom page omit "Don't try to pull the bed clothes over my eyes." 5th line from bottom of page omit "Every." 4th line from bottom of page omit entirely.

P. 44. 3rd line from bottom of page omit "God," substitute "Heavens."

P. 47. 3rd and 4th lines from top of page omit "In somebody's bed." 16th line from top of page omit "incestuous." 15th line from bottom of page omit "raping," substitute "making love to."

P. 48. 16th line from bottom of page omit "when Banjo." 15th, 14th, 13th and 12th lines from bottom of page omit entirely.

P. 49. 19th line from bottom of page omit dialogue, substitute "My Heavens, that's Bottomley to the life." 18th line from bottom omit entirely. 13th line from bottom of page omit "Damn it."

P. 50. Top line omit "damn," substitute "dear!"

P. 51. 18th line from bottom of page omit "God," substitute "Heaven!" Last line on page omit "that has to."

P. 52. Top line omit "have his diapers changed."

P. 53. 3d line from top of page omit "bitches," substitute "what a wonderful joke on." 17th line from top of page omit "God," substitute "Heaven."

P. 59. 24th line from top of page omit "Great God," substitute "Good Heavens."

P. 60. 2d line from top of page omit "damnedest," substitute "darnedest." 6th line from bottom of page omit "God," substitute "Heavens." 2nd line from bottom of page omit "Hell," substitute "Heck." Bottom line omit "Oh, God!"

P. 61. 2nd line from top of page omit "Oh, God! Oh, God!" 6th line from top of page omit "you." 7th line from top of page omit "French bitch —God damn it."

P. 62. By a little rearrangement, Bert need not bring in the tray of drinks. But note that no drinks are used in scene.

P. 63. 5th line from top of page omit "God's," substitute "Pete's."

P. 65. 20th line from bottom of page omit "a loud," substitute "an enthusiastic." 19th line from bottom of page omit "a," substitute "rather excited." 18th line from bottom of page omit "little high." 17th line from bottom of page omit "I'm a." 16th line from bottom omit "little high, but I can explain everything." 13th line from bottom of page omit "I read her the play and she thinks it's wonderful." 9th line from bottom of page omit "don't you," substitute "Have you been drinking?" 8th line from bottom of page omit "biggest day of my life. I know I'm a little drunk," substitute "I'm all excited though; I don't need alcohol." 7th line from bottom of page omit "but," capitalize "This." Same line, omit "In Billy's Tavern," substitute "in the hotel lobby." 6th line from bottom of page omit "night," substitute "evening." Same line omit "it was daylight until it was daylight," substitute "how late it was."

P. 66. 10th line from top of page omit "isn't that wonder-." 11th line from top omit "ful?" Same line omit "Well, we're." 12th line omit entirely. 14th line from top of page omit "some black coffee and." 15th line from top of page omit "care of." 21st line from top of page omit "Let's climb down a couple of chimneys." 23rd line from top of page omit "Hell," substitute "daylights."

P. 67. 13th line from bottom of page omit entirely. 10th line from bottom of page omit "Don't be afraid of my passion. Kiss me." 5th line from bottom of page omit "God's," substitute "Heaven's."

P. 68. 2nd line from top of page omit "Slaps Miss Preen's fanny." 17th line from top of page omit "brassiere," substitute "slipper." 17th line from bottom of page omit "Where the hell's," substitute "Where's." Last line on page omit "God," substitute "Jumpin' Jupiter."

P. 69. 8th line from top of page omit "Old hot pants," substitute "Oh-ho." 11th line from top of page omit "rewrite," substitute "work on the play." 13th line from bottom of page omit "bat out of hell," substitute "streak." 11th line from bottom of page omit "Fanny or whatever it is." Last line on page omit "damned," substitute "darned."

P. 70. 3rd line from top of page omit "oh, damn, damn, damn," substitute "Confound it all!" 4th line from top of page omit "Hell and damnation!"

P. 72. 19th line from bottom of page omit "God damnedest," substitute "most extraordinary."

P. 74. 12th line from bottom of page omit "How's the mattress business, Lorraine?" 11th and 10th lines omit entirely. 9th line omit "Banjo (c.) You've got me there, Mama."

P. 75. 13th line from top of page omit "all." 14th line from top of page omit entirely, substitute "(Banjo crosses D.L. Lorraine rises, crosses." 14th line from bottom of page omit "God," substitute "Goodness."

P. 76. 3rd line from top of page omit "God," substitute "Gosh."

P. 78. 16th line from bottom of page omit "hell of a," substitute "terrific." 14th line from bottom of page omit "damnedest," substitute "most poisonous."

P. 79. 2nd line from bottom of page omit "God's," substitute "Pete's."
P. 80. 6th line from top of page omit "God damn it!"

NEW PLAYS

★ **MOTHERHOOD OUT LOUD by Leslie Ayvazian, Brooke Berman, David Cale, Jessica Goldberg, Beth Henley, Lameece Issaq, Claire LaZebnik, Lisa Loomer, Michele Lowe, Marco Pennette, Theresa Rebeck, Luanne Rice, Annie Weisman and Cheryl L. West, conceived by Susan R. Rose and Joan Stein.** When entrusting the subject of motherhood to such a dazzling collection of celebrated American writers, what results is a joyous, moving, hilarious, and altogether thrilling theatrical event. "Never fails to strike both the funny bone and the heart." *–BackStage.* "Packed with wisdom, laughter, and plenty of wry surprises." *–TheaterMania.* [1M, 3W] ISBN: 978-0-8222-2589-8

★ **COCK by Mike Bartlett.** When John takes a break from his boyfriend, he accidentally meets the girl of his dreams. Filled with guilt and indecision, he decides there is only one way to straighten this out. "[A] brilliant and blackly hilarious feat of provocation." *–Independent.* "A smart, prickly and rewarding view of sexual and emotional confusion." *–Evening Standard.* [3M, 1W] ISBN: 978-0-8222-2766-3

★ **F. Scott Fitzgerald's THE GREAT GATSBY adapted for the stage by Simon Levy.** Jay Gatsby, a self-made millionaire, passionately pursues the elusive Daisy Buchanan. Nick Carraway, a young newcomer to Long Island, is drawn into their world of obsession, greed and danger. "Levy's combination of narration, dialogue and action delivers most of what is best in the novel." *–Seattle Post-Intelligencer.* "A beautifully crafted interpretation of the 1925 novel which defined the Jazz Age." *–London Free Press.* [5M, 4W] ISBN: 978-0-8222-2727-4

★ **LONELY, I'M NOT by Paul Weitz.** At an age when most people are discovering what they want to do with their lives, Porter has been married and divorced, earned seven figures as a corporate "ninja," and had a nervous breakdown. It's been four years since he's had a job or a date, and he's decided to give life another shot. "Critic's pick!" *–NY Times.* "An enjoyable ride." *–NY Daily News.* [3M, 3W] ISBN: 978-0-8222-2734-2

★ **ASUNCION by Jesse Eisenberg.** Edgar and Vinny are not racist. In fact, Edgar maintains a blog condemning American imperialism, and Vinny is three-quarters into a Ph.D. in Black Studies. When Asuncion becomes their new roommate, the boys have a perfect opportunity to demonstrate how open-minded they truly are. "Mr. Eisenberg writes lively dialogue that strikes plenty of comic sparks." *–NY Times.* "An almost ridiculously enjoyable portrait of slacker trauma among would-be intellectuals." *–Newsday.* [2M, 2W] ISBN: 978-0-8222-2630-7

DRAMATISTS PLAY SERVICE, INC.
440 Park Avenue South, New York, NY 10016 212-683-8960 Fax 212-213-1539
postmaster@dramatists.com   www.dramatists.com

NEW PLAYS

★ **THE PICTURE OF DORIAN GRAY by Roberto Aguirre-Sacasa, based on the novel by Oscar Wilde.** Preternaturally handsome Dorian Gray has his portrait painted by his college classmate Basil Hallwood. When their mutual friend Henry Wotton offers to include it in a show, Dorian makes a fateful wish—that his portrait should grow old instead of him—and strikes an unspeakable bargain with the devil. [5M, 2W] ISBN: 978-0-8222-2590-4

★ **THE LYONS by Nicky Silver.** As Ben Lyons lies dying, it becomes clear that he and his wife have been at war for many years, and his impending demise has brought no relief. When they're joined by their children all efforts at a sentimental goodbye to the dying patriarch are soon abandoned. "Hilariously frank, clear-sighted, compassionate and forgiving." *–NY Times.* "Mordant, dark and rich." *–Associated Press.* [3M, 3W] ISBN: 978-0-8222-2659-8

★ **STANDING ON CEREMONY by Mo Gaffney, Jordan Harrison, Moisés Kaufman, Neil LaBute, Wendy MacLeod, José Rivera, Paul Rudnick, and Doug Wright, conceived by Brian Shnipper.** Witty, warm and occasionally wacky, these plays are vows to the blessings of equality, the universal challenges of relationships and the often hilarious power of love. "CEREMONY puts a human face on a hot-button issue and delivers laughter and tears rather than propaganda." *–BackStage.* [3M, 3W] ISBN: 978-0-8222-2654-3

★ **ONE ARM by Moisés Kaufman, based on the short story and screenplay by Tennessee Williams.** Ollie joins the Navy and becomes the lightweight boxing champion of the Pacific Fleet. Soon after, he loses his arm in a car accident, and he turns to hustling to survive. "[A] fast, fierce, brutally beautiful stage adaptation." *–NY Magazine.* "A fascinatingly lurid, provocative and fatalistic piece of theater." *–Variety.* [7M, 1W] ISBN: 978-0-8222-2564-5

★ **AN ILIAD by Lisa Peterson and Denis O'Hare.** A modern-day retelling of Homer's classic. Poetry and humor, the ancient tale of the Trojan War and the modern world collide in this captivating theatrical experience. "Shocking, glorious, primal and deeply satisfying." *–Time Out NY.* "Explosive, altogether breathtaking." *–Chicago Sun-Times.* [1M] ISBN: 978-0-8222-2687-1

★ **THE COLUMNIST by David Auburn.** At the height of the Cold War, Joe Alsop is the nation's most influential journalist, beloved, feared and courted by the Washington world. But as the '60s dawn and America undergoes dizzying change, the intense political dramas Joe is embroiled in become deeply personal as well. "Intensely satisfying." *–Bloomberg News.* [5M, 2W] ISBN: 978-0-8222-2699-4

DRAMATISTS PLAY SERVICE, INC.
440 Park Avenue South, New York, NY 10016 212-683-8960 Fax 212-213-1539
postmaster@dramatists.com   www.dramatists.com

NEW PLAYS

★ **BENGAL TIGER AT THE BAGHDAD ZOO by Rajiv Joseph.** The lives of two American Marines and an Iraqi translator are forever changed by an encounter with a quick-witted tiger who haunts the streets of war-torn Baghdad. "[A] boldly imagined, harrowing and surprisingly funny drama." *–NY Times.* "Tragic yet darkly comic and highly imaginative." *–CurtainUp.* [5M, 2W] ISBN: 978-0-8222-2565-2

★ **THE PITMEN PAINTERS by Lee Hall, inspired by a book by William Feaver.** Based on the triumphant true story, a group of British miners discover a new way to express themselves and unexpectedly become art-world sensations. "Excitingly ambiguous, in-the-moment theater." *–NY Times.* "Heartfelt, moving and deeply politicized." *–Chicago Tribune.* [5M, 2W] ISBN: 978-0-8222-2507-2

★ **RELATIVELY SPEAKING by Ethan Coen, Elaine May and Woody Allen.** In TALKING CURE, Ethan Coen uncovers the sort of insanity that can only come from family. Elaine May explores the hilarity of passing in GEORGE IS DEAD. In HONEYMOON MOTEL, Woody Allen invites you to the sort of wedding day you won't forget. "Firecracker funny." *–NY Times.* "A rollicking good time." *–New Yorker.* [8M, 7W] ISBN: 978-0-8222-2394-8

★ **SONS OF THE PROPHET by Stephen Karam.** If to live is to suffer, then Joseph Douaihy is more alive than most. With unexplained chronic pain and the fate of his reeling family on his shoulders, Joseph's health, sanity, and insurance premium are on the line. "Explosively funny." *–NY Times.* "At once deep, deft and beautifully made." *–New Yorker.* [5M, 3W] ISBN: 978-0-8222-2597-3

★ **THE MOUNTAINTOP by Katori Hall.** A gripping reimagination of events the night before the assassination of the civil rights leader Dr. Martin Luther King, Jr. "An ominous electricity crackles through the opening moments." *–NY Times.* "[A] thrilling, wild, provocative flight of magical realism." *–Associated Press.* "Crackles with theatricality and a humanity more moving than sainthood." *–NY Newsday.* [1M, 1W] ISBN: 978-0-8222-2603-1

★ **ALL NEW PEOPLE by Zach Braff.** Charlie is 35, heartbroken, and just wants some time away from the rest of the world. Long Beach Island seems to be the perfect escape until his solitude is interrupted by a motley parade of misfits who show up and change his plans. "Consistently and sometimes sensationally funny." *–NY Times.* "A morbidly funny play about the trendy new existential condition of being young, adorable, and miserable." *–Variety.* [2M, 2W] ISBN: 978-0-8222-2562-1

DRAMATISTS PLAY SERVICE, INC.
440 Park Avenue South, New York, NY 10016 212-683-8960 Fax 212-213-1539
postmaster@dramatists.com www.dramatists.com

NEW PLAYS

★ **CLYBOURNE PARK by Bruce Norris.** WINNER OF THE 2011 PULITZER PRIZE AND 2012 TONY AWARD. Act One takes place in 1959 as community leaders try to stop the sale of a home to a black family. Act Two is set in the same house in the present day as the now predominantly African-American neighborhood battles to hold its ground. "Vital, sharp-witted and ferociously smart." *–NY Times.* "A theatrical treasure…Indisputably, uproariously funny." *–Entertainment Weekly.* [4M, 3W] ISBN: 978-0-8222-2697-0

★ **WATER BY THE SPOONFUL by Quiara Alegría Hudes.** WINNER OF THE 2012 PULITZER PRIZE. A Puerto Rican veteran is surrounded by the North Philadelphia demons he tried to escape in the service. "This is a very funny, warm, and yes uplifting play." *–Hartford Courant.* "The play is a combination poem, prayer and app on how to cope in an age of uncertainty, speed and chaos." *–Variety.* [4M, 3W] ISBN: 978-0-8222-2716-8

★ **RED by John Logan.** WINNER OF THE 2010 TONY AWARD. Mark Rothko has just landed the biggest commission in the history of modern art. But when his young assistant, Ken, gains the confidence to challenge him, Rothko faces the agonizing possibility that his crowning achievement could also become his undoing. "Intense and exciting." *–NY Times.* "Smart, eloquent entertainment." *–New Yorker.* [2M] ISBN: 978-0-8222-2483-9

★ **VENUS IN FUR by David Ives.** Thomas, a beleaguered playwright/director, is desperate to find an actress to play Vanda, the female lead in his adaptation of the classic sadomasochistic tale *Venus in Fur.* "Ninety minutes of good, kinky fun." *–NY Times.* "A fast-paced journey into one man's entrapment by a clever, vengeful female." *–Associated Press.* [1M, 1W] ISBN: 978-0-8222-2603-1

★ **OTHER DESERT CITIES by Jon Robin Baitz.** Brooke returns home to Palm Springs after a six-year absence and announces that she is about to publish a memoir dredging up a pivotal and tragic event in the family's history—a wound they don't want reopened. "Leaves you feeling both moved and gratifyingly sated." *–NY Times.* "A genuine pleasure." *–NY Post.* [2M, 3W] ISBN: 978-0-8222-2605-5

★ **TRIBES by Nina Raine.** Billy was born deaf into a hearing family and adapts brilliantly to his family's unconventional ways, but it's not until he meets Sylvia, a young woman on the brink of deafness, that he finally understands what it means to be understood. "A smart, lively play." *–NY Times.* "[A] bright and boldly provocative drama." *–Associated Press.* [3M, 2W] ISBN: 978-0-8222-2751-9

DRAMATISTS PLAY SERVICE, INC.
440 Park Avenue South, New York, NY 10016 212-683-8960 Fax 212-213-1539
postmaster@dramatists.com   www.dramatists.com